Travel & the Single Male

Temple of the Single Truth

TRAVEL & THE SINGLE MALE

Bruce Cassirer

TSM PUBLISHING

CHANNEL ISLAND, CALIFORNIA

Publisher's Note

The recommendations in this book have been made according to the author's tastes and personal style. He has not received payment, or compensation in any form from the airlines, car rental agencies, hotels, restaurants, or any facilities recommended in this book.

Neither the author nor the publisher assume any responsibility for the travel arrangements, decisions, or sexual choices made by readers. Additionally, please be aware that, in the world of travel, everything can change: prices, phone numbers, availability of car rentals, rooms, and so on. The author has made every attempt to assure the accuracy of the information contained in this book, but cannot assume responsibility for any typographical errors, omissions, or changes.

TSM Publishing
Suite #122
3600 S. Harbor Blvd.
Channel Island, CA 93035

ISBN 0-9634234-0-1
Printed in the United States of America

Contents

TABLE OF MAPS

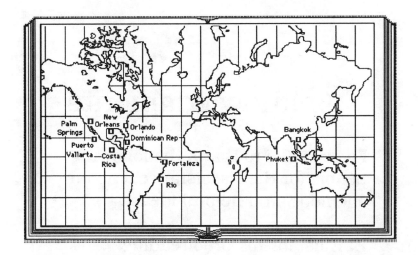

Acknowledgments

I would like to thank the following people for their assistance, encouragement, and helpful ideas:

El Ellis, for his proofreading
Manyu Chan, for her assistance in
    research
Ilse Frank, for her encouragement,
    support, and being my mom
Kenneth Blaustein, for his typesetting
    assistance
Rick Benzel, the man who helped me
    make this into a book

Preface

I love to travel. I feel cheated when I have to go to the airport and drop someone off: I want to go too. I have traveled since I was a child. My parents, who came from Europe, made my brother, my sister, and me feel that traveling was a special reward in life. They were right. Our only problem was that my parents wanted the trips to be educational, my sister liked romantic hideaways, my brother searched out the coldest places he could find, and I . . . I only wanted a warm beach. Now I am in my early forties and have been retired for about eight years, having had the good fortune to make some prosperous investments in real estate. I have traveled the world extensively looking for that perfect beach and sunny clime.

In planning my trips, however, I noticed that whenever I went to bookstores I could find essentially only two kinds of travel books. One kind was written for the backpacker type, and contained information about the cheapest hotels, restaurants, and airfares; the other kind seemed to be for the idle rich, with reviews and tips about only the most deluxe hotels, the best restaurants, and the places where the locals will least likely get in your way.

Neither of these kinds of guides was for me, nor, I suspected, for many other men who felt as I do. I wanted to find out about the honestly great places, where men could learn something new, have some adventure, and quite possibly meet some women. And so I have written this guide.

Travel and the Single Male

This travel book will take you to those places that are made for single, independent, inquisitive, and mildly affluent males. It is for men who desire something different, have some money, and are single—or at least still have a single disposition. For this kind of man, going to Hawaii, Cancun, or a Club Med is not the answer to his feelings of travel lust. If you're like me, you don't want simply to lie poolside next to strangers, or to spend your time searching out nude beaches or trying to sound clever in bars and discos just to buy a girl a drink. You want fun, adventure, and lusty potential.

We'll start with some simple trips, not too far from home and fairly comfortable. These trips will help you if you are not used to traveling alone. Then we'll take some trips that are more distant, interesting, and exotic. These are places where the women will chase and fight over you, and your biggest problem will not be *who* but *when*. These are places where being an American male is a pleasure, the beaches aren't only for tourists and aren't polluted, the hotels are reasonable, the environment exciting, young women are appreciative, and you are a KING.

THE GOLDEN RULES OF TRAVEL

Before we begin, let me assure you that I've actually stayed at most of the hotels described here, used the car rental agencies, relaxed and flirted on the beaches, and fallen in love in the bars I've recommended. This book is written from my real experiences. Let me therefore relate to you a few of the basic rules I consider important to this kind of travel:

Travel Solo   My friends ask how I can travel alone so much. Don't I get lonely, scared, bored, confused, tongue-tied? Of course I do! But that is what makes traveling an experience.

Vacationing solo means you have to make your own new friends, plan your own day, and face the chance of being lonely. I have found that when I travel with friends, I use them for my entertainment and rely on them for excitement. Because I'm basically shy, I often remain in the background while my friends make things happen and do the socializing. But I always have a better time when I'm traveling alone since I'm forced to be friendly, adventurous, and learn to enjoy myself. I've also outgrown sharing rooms, splitting meal expenses, and being afraid of the unknown.

As much as you can, make traveling alone your preferred style. It will help you to appreciate and understand yourself.

A last thought on this topic is a quote from Eugene Fodor, the famous travel author: "The joy of travel should not be derived solely from seeing the sights but from mingling with peoples whose customs, habits, and general outlook are different from your own."

Don't expect to fall in love One of the main enticements of travel is meeting new women. But just as you don't expect to fall in love on every date, don't spend your time looking for that perfect woman to sweep you off your feet or to bring back home.

Granted it would be the picture perfect conclusion for some men to fall in love while on vacation in the south of France, on the deck of a Greek cruise ship, or on the back seat of a gondola in Venice . . . but that's unlikely for most of us on short vacations. To go away expecting to find love usually interfers with simply having a good time.

Leave Your Cultural Blinders Home Outside our country, many things change. What is legal and moral here is quite different elsewhere. In the rest of the world, sexual attitudes can be quite different: women friends may walk holding hands and men may kiss each other hello, both without any of the sexual overtones we usually ascribe to these actions.

At some of the destinations in this book, the "working girls" in the bars and massage parlors are what many people would consider prostitutes. In some cases, yes, you do pay for sex with them, but in other cases, their interests are in meeting a good man, having good food and a nice hotel room, and improving their lot in life. Some of these women are everyday college students, models, or sales ladies who, if they had been born in different circumstances, might be faithful and trustworthy wives. In short, I believe that cultures can be so different that we cannot judge a book by its cover. If you treat these women with kindness and respect, you'll be surprised what great friends they become. For example, on my last visit in Phuket, Thailand, the girls at my favorite bar gave me a bouquet of flowers and a special gift in appreciation of my loyalty to their bar and for being a good friend to them.

Nevertheless, let me add that you should always follow what I call the "used car" principle: never buy a used car you haven't driven. This analogy should apply to your travels at all times, from selecting a hotel room, to trying a new dish in a restaurant, to spending time with a new woman. If you feel unsure, always look at a room before you pay, taste a sample before you eat, and never give a woman the payment before the service. I don't mean to sound tactless, but this advice will help you avoid many frustrating and anxious moments.

I can recall one incident in Chiang Mai, in northern Thailand. I thought a beautiful young woman I met couldn't resist my charms and good looks, but in reality she just wanted an air-conditioned room with a television. Despite my attempts at reason, I had to get the security guard to remove her.

So, whether you're in a bar, a massage parlor, a disco, or on the street, follow the used car principle and remember: nothing is free.

Use Protection   There seems never to be enough reminders about this topic. Most foreign women actually will be more worried about what diseases you may have. They apparently consider that Americans in general are carriers of AIDS and feel that most infections come from us. They may be leery of you and want to get to know you better, so take your time with a new acquaintance. Buy her a drink and get to know her.   *See appendix for more information on sexual diseases.*

Watch out for Murphy's Law   When traveling, whatever you don't expect often happens, and that which you most expect doesn't. On my last trip to Orlando with some friends, our flight connection from Memphis to Florida was canceled, and by the time we arrived three hours late, the agent at the Hertz counter informed us that our car had already been rented. "Oh shit, what do we do now?" we lamented. Fortunately, the agent said that since they were out of compacts and intermediates, we would get a new Lincoln towncar for the price of a compact. Well, this good luck set the tone for the whole trip. I had the car for three weeks and paid practically nothing.

On the other hand, I've also had many less gratifying outcomes, such as the time I was arriving in Honolulu from Asia. I had been among the first to check my luggage at the airport, and as a result, my bags were the last off from a 747 that had over four hundred people on it. By the time I got my bags, went through customs, and got to my hotel, half a day had gone by and the sun had set. The only room I could get was one that faced a brick wall. Then, on my way to the room, I ran into a guy I met on the flight. He had just barely caught the plane in Asia, but since his bags were last on, they were first off. He was already coming back from a swim and he wanted to show me his ocean-front room!

When traveling, be prepared for the worst, the best, and the unpredictable to occur. Make it a game to see who wins, you or Murphy.

Reconfirm This advice sounds simple, yet for a truly relaxing and uncomplicated trip, it's a must. While in Bangkok last year, I made a quick change of schedule to go to Manila on Korean Airlines. On my return to Bangkok, I called Korean to reconfirm my flight home to Los Angeles, but the agent on the phone had never heard of me and said my seat was gone. Whoever changed my schedule had failed to put the change in the computer. Not only did I have to go to their office with my ticket, but I had to take a three-stop flight home that took thirty-five hours.

Don't be lazy or over-confident in our new electronic marvels; computers are only as good as the people who type the data! Remember: don't take anything for granted: reconfirm every reservation.

Travel and the Single Male

Shop by phone   My best friend was recently disappointed when his plans to go to Cancun, Mexico were botched by a travel agent. He explained to me that Mexicana Airline had offered a $99 promotional ticket to anywhere in Mexico, but instead of calling himself, he asked his travel agent to make the arrangements. However, she wrote down the wrong dates and went off on her own trip. By the time she returned, the promotion had ended.

I don't mean to suggest at all that travel agents are bad, but it's worthwhile to do your own homework and make a few calls. I recommend reading the Sunday papers, such as the Los Angeles Times, the New York Times, the San Francisco Chronicle, and the Miami Herald, where you can discover all sorts of special deals, promotions, and discounts.

Another reason to make your own reservations is that fares and availability change frequently. Last year, an average of 11,982 schedule changes and 215,396 fare changes were processed **daily** for 724 airlines by Official Airline Guide, the travel information company. Since it can take a few days for new fares to get programmed into the travel agents' computers, you can lose out on the chance to get a discount seat as only a select few are allowed on most flights. It's better to make your own reservations or, if you prefer, you can give the locator number to your agent if you want him or her to issue you the tickets. In fact, I pay a flat fee to my travel agent to issue tickets and vouchers, but I do all the research and reservations myself.

For those of you with computers and modems, you can use one of the database services such as CompuServe or Prodigy to make all your airline, hotel, and car reservations. In fact, by doing this, you tap into the same reservation systems as travel agents, Sabre, run by American Airlines. You can compare prices, check schedules, and even look at a seating diagram of your aircraft.

If you don't have access to your own computer system, there are three ways to make hotel reservations: use the central toll-free number, call direct to the specific hotel you want, or book a reservation through a trusted travel agent. But according to a recent report from the Condé Nast magazine *Traveler*, calling directly to the hotel is best as prices can be up to 40 percent higher if you use an agent. Their recommendation: "The best bet is to find a travel agent who is in equal parts a computer wizard, frequent flier mileage juggler, telephone jockey, and newspaper scanner." Since such an agent is nearly impossible to find, why not do it yourself?

If you decide to use a consolidator—sellers of those cheap tickets you see advertised in the Sunday travel sections of major papers—then take a precaution by checking directly with the airline involved to confirm that a reservation has been made in your name on the promised flight before you make your full payment!

Travel Light One way to avoid the nightmare of having your luggage come off last is obviously to travel light. You'll be surprised how much you don't need, and pleased by not having to go through the baggage chaos.

To take luggage on-board, Samsonite makes a wonderful carry-on that fits under your seat. This piece has a hard shell like a regular suitcase, wheels, and a retractable handle that allows you to carry a second hand-bag hassle free. Use a garment bag as a second piece of carry-on luggage. It usually fits in the over-head bins, or the flight attendant will hang it in business class if the coach bins are full.

For your packing plans, remember that underseat storage is approximately 45 inches, measured as the sum total of length, width, and depth of your carry-on piece. The maximum size that fits in an overhead-bin is about 60 inches, measured in the dimensions of 36 inches X 14 inches X 10 inches. Airline personnel can use discretion in allowing luggage in the cabin, especially if the flight is not full, so smile and be polite if you are in a jam.

Pay Attention to Your Money Money is like sex: you never know how much is enough; you are usually totally confused by the exchange rate; the more you have, the more you want; and once you lose it, you want it even more. I suggest you take advantage of a technological solution: -

Travel and the Single Male

Automatic Teller Machines (ATMs). Rather than taking a lot of cash with you, simply get more when you need it. Obviously the less you have, the less you can spend, but also the less you can lose or have stolen.

Twice I have lost a large sum of money—once on a street in Japan and once on a beach in Brazil where I had fallen asleep and discovered upon awakening that my bag, tennis shoes, and tee-shirt had all disappeared.

There is no need to carry a large amount of cash or traveler's checks, which are lousy in receiving good exchange rates. The Cirrus, Plus, and Interlink ATM systems are available almost everywhere in the world, and they give exchange rates reserved for large business transactions. Except where the exchange rate is set by the government, ATMs generally convert at the commercial rate set for transactions of one million dollars or more.

Note though that ATMs outside North America do not accept personal identification numbers (PINs) longer than four digits, and that the keypads on many foreign ATMs do not include letters. So, if you think of your PIN as a word, convert it to the corresponding numbers prior to departure. I also recommend that you leave money in your home checking account, as foreign ATM's often don't have the ability to tap into credit lines.

When traveling through airports, hotels, or strange streets, separate your valuables. For example, put your money in your billfold, your passport and tickets in a carry-on bag, and your credit cards and copies of tickets and passport in an inside shoulder harness, available in most luggage stores. You never know when something can be stolen. When I returned from my last trip to Brazil, I somehow lost my passport at the airport in Miami. While in line at the Federal Building in Los Angeles, I asked the guy in front of me why he was there. He replied, "I just returned from a trip to South America and someone stole my passport in Miami."

Do as the Romans do   When you are in foreign lands, try to be as inconspicuous as possible. Don't wear your suit on the boardwalk in Rio with your Rolex watch and gold chains exposed. You are only asking to be singled out as a rich, showy American and that can lead to trouble, or simply embarrassment. One time in the Philippines, I was going to an office of Singapore Airlines (which without a doubt has the prettiest stewardesses of all airlines, and was named "World's Best Airline" for 1991 by Condé Nast magazine). I was in the business district of Makati, and as I got out of the cab, everyone began pointing and laughing at me. Although it was 90 degrees and 98% humidity, normal dress for men is pants, shirt, and dress shoes, but I was wearing running shorts and tennis shoes. I'm sure I was charged double by the taxi driver for being an arrogant American.

On the other hand, the suit and Rolex watch can be useful if you are trying to get a special favor, such as an upgrade on your airline when you don't deserve it. For instance, on my last trip from Costa Rica to Miami, I was sharply dressed and that helped me to convince the ticket agent that I should be in first class when I asserted that I had enough miles in their frequent flyer program. I didn't, but I looked the part, and so he didn't argue it with me.

Travel off-season   If you travel off-season, you miss the crowds, the prices drop 50 percent, and the local people even come out. Two years ago, I made the mistake of traveling to Bangkok during the busy Christmas season and was forced to pay $200 a night at the Sheraton Royal Orchid, one of the world's greatest hotels. Two months later I got the same room for 30 percent less.

On the other hand, you need to pick your off-season well. If you go to southern Thailand in June or July, you practically need a boat with you, and few people—aside from me—enjoy Palm Springs in August when it can reach 120 degrees.

The key is to go during "shoulder" season, that brief period of time between high and low season where the prices have come down, the weather is usually pretty good, and most people are gone. Below is a list of shoulder seasons:

Travel and the Single Male

Asia:	early November, and April through early May
South America:	September through November (their spring)
Caribbean:	from April 15 until June; early November
Costa Rica:	None; it rains nine months of the year. But stay away from Christmas and New Years. The best time is during March.
California Deserts:	Late March and April are magnificent; *(avoid college student spring break in mid-April)* Also late September and early October.
Florida:	avoid major holidays and school vacation periods.

There are two useful 900 numbers that will give you one-to- ten-day advance weather forecasts for any city in the world. Call American Express at 1-900-WEATHER (75 cents per minute) or USA Today at 1-900-933-3000 (95 cents per minute).

Don't Spend Money in Airports   Don't buy anything at an airport unless it is absolutely necessary. Airports must be one of those places in the world where rip-offs are legal. I've bought awful hot dogs for five dollars, paid mysterious taxes on airport entrances and exits, and have been herded into duty-free shops for those one-of-a-kind bargains. I've never bought anything in a duty-free shop that I couldn't buy cheaper at K-Mart. I even bring my own food, papers, and magazines when I travel. One time as I walked out of customs, I was told I *had* to buy an unofficial duplicate passport so I could put mine in a safe and carry the extra for identification. This was not a bad idea, but it cost me $20.

Sometimes it seems that the main function of an airport is to give you a place to spend that last bit of foreign currency. If you have currency left over, I recommend that you simply go to the airport gift shop and buy Kodak film, something useful, standardized, and usually priced reasonably.

Airports are busiest Monday and Thursday for business travelers and Friday and Sunday for vacationers. Try to book flights that do not leave during rush hours 7:00 A.M. to 9:00 A.M. and 4:00 P.M. to 6:00 P.M. These are the times when you sit on the runway behind ten other planes waiting to take off.

Join the clubs Imagine checking in at the airport at the first class counter, having priority baggage handling, preselected seats, and a choice of specially ordered meals on the plane. Then when your flight is over, you stroll leisurely to the car-rental firm, by-pass the lines, and get on the bus to the parking lot where you are dropped at your car with the keys waiting in the ignition. At your hotel, you get a free upgrade to an ocean-front room with a free newspaper and a basket of fresh fruit. Does this seem like Fantasy Island? All these extras are free for the taking just by joining the clubs.

The Northwest Perks Program is one example. As a member, after you've flown 20,000 frequent flyer miles you receive a free coach ticket to any destination city they fly to in the United States; at 40,000 miles, you get a free coach ticket to any of their destination cities in Europe. And on many of their new routes to Asia, Northwest includes automatic enrollment and a free domestic round-trip ticket. The United Airlines program offers a free trip to Asia at 50,000 miles. It's even better when you fly during the off-season when the airlines often offer triple miles for a flight.

For hotels, by joining the Sheraton Club you can reserve the cheapest room and, if availabile, upgrade to the most deluxe or superior room for the same price. Joining Avis Wizard or Hertz Number One club gives you instant check-in and car-rental, as well as bonus miles for some airlines. For instance, I live about sixty miles from LAX and rather than asking a friend to pick me up from one of my trips, I rent a car with unlimited mileage and free drop off for less than the cost of an airport bus and a short taxi ride. I also receive 500 miles credit on my frequent-flyer program. Since I take two or more trips a year, these frequent-flyer programs eventually pay for a free trip.

I'm currently arranging a trip to Europe and selling a free ticket to a friend, which helps to pay for my trip. In addition, now that I've flown 30,000 miles, I can belong to the Platinum Club and get upgraded to business or first class for free if a seat is available. Another program just initiated is the American Express Frequent Flyer mileage for any purpose. Once you join the club, all charges on your American Express Card can be converted to credit on any of the seven major airlines.

Stay Informed Read and then read some more. Today there are many specials, bargains, discounts and even sales for the aware traveler. Waiting until some airline advertises double or triple miles on a new route will mean a free trip the following year. In addition to the American Express magazine *Travel & Leisure* and Condé Nast's *Traveler*, there are two newsletters that can keep you informed: *Consumer Reports Travel Letter:* (Box 53629, Boulder CO, 80322-3629 or call 800-999-7959. $37 per year) and *Travel Smart*, Communication House, Inc. 40 Beechdale Road, Dobbs Ferry, NY 10522. $44 per year).

Following these golden rules will not guarantee a great trip, but they will minimize the hassles, frustrations, and confusion. Remember that the two greatest gifts God has given you are an American passport and good health. Take advantage of these. Traveling is an adventure, a test of your skills and wits. Make it a game, have fun, and play to win (women)!

Part 1
Short and Fun

- **New Orleans**
- **Orlando**
- **Palm Springs**
- **Puerto Vallarta**

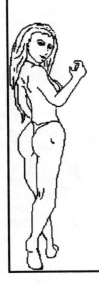

New Orleans

No other city in the United States is quite like New Orleans. In fact, when I'm there, I feel like I'm not in the United States at all. I love its music, its food, its setting, its decor, its history, its architecture, and its people with their strange accent. This is the perfect city for the single male to explore — lustful, hedonistic, and yet romantic.

GETTING THERE

New Orleans International Airport is about twelve miles west of New Orleans proper and is served by most domestic airlines. The city is compact, so that renting a car is not necessary. New Orleans is meant to be traversed by foot, and after a taxi to your hotel, no other transportation is needed. However, if you are lazy you'll pay $5 for a taxi ride in the Quarter and maybe double that to uptown restaurants and Audubon Park. On the other hand, renting a car is recommended if you would like to take a drive down the coast to Biloxi, Mississippi, a great way to extend your trip.

ABOUT THE CITY

If you truly want to see this city in all its majesty, for a few dollars you can take the deluxe glass elevator to the top of the thirty-one-story World Trade Center on Canal Street. From the observation deck, you'll see riverside, lakeside, downriver (downtown), upriver (uptown), and the tree-lined Canal Street which divides the city. To the right of Canal Street is the French Quarter with the steeples of St. Louis

Chapter 1

Cathedral rising above the roof lines; to the left of Canal Street is the central business district; and way off on the horizon is Lake Pontchartrain.

New Orleans lies on the east bank of the Mississippi River about 100 miles from the Gulf of Mexico. Often called the Paris of America, it combines old French charm with the hustle of a modern commercial and thriving American city. At one time or another, the French, the Spanish, the Confederate, and the American flag has flown here. In 1762, the French gave Spain the Louisiana Territory, but in 1800 Napoleon forced Spain to give it back. In 1803, the U. S. government purchased New Orleans and all of the Louisiana Territory from France. In 1812, Andrew Jackson defeated the British at the Battle of New Orleans. Much of the architecture is French Colonial, evident in the famous Vieux Square, where the first French settlers lived in fortified squares. No other American city bears the mark of foreign cultures as much as New Orleans.

The intermingling of the Spanish families and traditions with the Caribbean slaves created the present day Creole culture. Prior to the Civil war, slavery provided prosperity for the locals, but the opulent life style ended with the end of the war. By the early 20th century, gambling and prostitution became prevalent and nearly 1,000 bars and bordellos existed! Not until the U. S. Navy threatened to abandon the city because the red light district was too much of a distraction did New Orleans decide to enforce its prostitution laws!

But what they couldn't outlaw was the music, the colorful atmosphere, and a live-and-let-be attitude. No other American city has celebrations like the Mardi Gras, a feast for the senses. No one notices or cares whether you're alone, married, or just out for a stroll. New Orleans is the perfect place for the single, adventurous male.

WHEN TO GO

In the summer months, suffocating heat, humidity and rain are common. Expect temperatures in the nineties. The only saving grace during this time of year is the night air; steamy and provocative, it is perfect for wonderful walks into the dark.

Fall and spring are cooler but also much more crowded. Shoulder seasons for New Orleans are early October or mid-April, giving you the best of both worlds. Take note, however, that the Sugar Bowl is New Year's day, the Jazz and Heritage Festival is in late April to early May, and Mardi Gras is in February on the day before Ash Wednesday. At these times, you will definitely need confirmed reservations. My favorite time to go to New Orleans is in early spring!

WHAT TO DO

No other city in the United States is more fun to walk than New Orleans. The main attraction of New Orleans is just browsing around the **French Quarter** (Vieux Carré) until some great food, music, women, or dancing stops you. The French Quarter covers about 70 square blocks between Canal Street and Rampart Street.

There are a few sights that you must see to make your trip more interesting and educational. Just take a slow walk, observe the buildings around you, and you'll go back a few hundred years in history. Enjoy the iron grillwork, the lacy balconies, and the aroma of freshly baked bread.

Jackson Square in the heart of the French Quarter is where historic public meetings and celebrations for returning heros once took place. Today it is a charming park surrounded by artisans and local merry makers. You might find an antique on adjacent Royal Street, or you can just sit down in Jackson Square to watch the mimes and artists

perform. Then stroll over to **Preservation Hall** at 726 St.
Peter Street to hear some jazz, but be prepared for crowds
and perhaps a wait.

Close by is the **French Market**, which occupies almost
four city blocks. Here you can choose from a variety of
fruits, vegetables, meats, and fish. You can also find cheap
sun-glasses and T-shirts in this bargain corner for the
thrifty tourist.

St. Louis Cathedral is one of the most famous and
beautiful churches in the country. It was completed in 1794
and is flanked by the Cabildo and the Presbyter buildings.
These structures now contain museums showing the
history of Louisiana, an art gallery and biweekly, visual
productions of local culture and national history. Within
the **Louisiana State Museum** complex is the restored
building that was the U.S. Mint from 1838 to 1861 at 400
Esplanade Ave. This building demonstrates the Victorian
and Classical architectural styles that were prevalent
during the American Revolution.

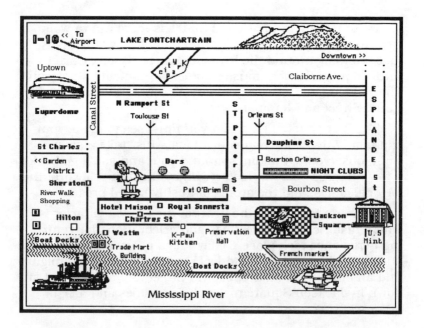

New Orleans

When you get tired, how about some Creole-style sea-food at **Galatoire** (209 Bourbon Street) for lunch or in the early evening? Some other good restaurants are **K-Paul Louisiana Kitchen** for Cajun food (416 Chartres Street) and **Antoine's** (713 St. Louis Street) for the French special. The Po'Boy sandwiches of fresh French bread are heavenly and available on almost every block.   Be sure to get some pralines, those delicious, old-fashioned New Orleans candies. A first bite puts you on a sugar high but from there on you are addicted and a tasting tour becomes part of your daily routine. Besides the roundish sweets there are Praline ice cream, cheese cake, sauces, and entire restaurants that only serve Praline permutations. The best places are the **Old Time Shop** (627 Royal Street) and **Aunt Sally's Original Creole Pralines** in the French Market (810 Decatur Street).

During the day the humidity and temperature may drive you inside. You might try some shopping at the uniquely structured, air-conditioned **River Walk** shopping center, the site of the 1984 World's Fair, across from the Hilton Hotel.

Try a river cruise on the paddlewheeler **Cajun Queen** or the **Creole Queen**, both of which depart from the Riverwalk dock. If you enjoy these trips, then you might want to take a 3- to 12-day cruise on the **Delta** or **Mississippi Queen** boats up the river. The front desk at your hotel usually can provide the latest departure times and locations.

Early morning runs through the French Quarter are possible because of the one-way traffic on some streets. This is a great way to spot boutiques, hidden stores, and little bakeries (my favorites) that you would ordinarily miss. You can return to these during your early evening stroll.

Remember when people say "downtown" they mean the area north of the French Quarter; "uptown" means the area upriver from Canal Street. A special treat is the eighty-cent trolley ride on the **St. Charles Avenue Line,** the oldest continuously operated streetcar line in the world. The double tracks run the length of St. Charles and provide a fascinating view of life in the Garden District and Uptown. You can board on Canal Street.

Chapter 1

If you are lazy and don't want to take the trolley ride (a round trip can take two hours) I suggested you take a cab through the **Garden District**, where you can see the oldest and largest homes in New Orleans surrounded by cobblestone streets with tiled name plates. The wrought-iron fences and mansion size homes put you back in time.

My favorite building is the new **Louisiana Superdome**, at 1500 Poydras Street. This twenty-seven-story structure is one of the largest indoor stadiums in the United States and can hold up to 90,000 people. A modern wonder of the world, it is especially fascinating to visit when it's empty and you can be in the middle of an enormous hollow bowl. Guided tours are available, but it's more fun to ramble around alone.

If you happen to be in New Orleans during the summer months, consider this suggestion: drive the 26-mile causeway across Lake Pontchartrain and take a walk in the pine forests to cool off! New Orleans is a walking town but sometimes the humidity can be truly unbearable and those cool drives, lake breezes, and river boat rides are the perfect remedy.

WHERE TO STAY

A few choices include small traditional inns, European-style hotels, or typical American large hotels. All have air conditioning, swimming pools, and courtyards. The prices range from $75.00 to $200.00 per night, depending on the season and availability. (Check to see if there are any conventions in town, as these can take up many of the choice rooms). The most interesting are:

Hotel Maison de Ville Total charm and ambiance with 23 units in the French Quarter, the area you want to be in. Tennesse Williams lived in unit #9. You can arrange your own French Quarter cottage with a private patio. 727 Toulouse Street (504-561-5858)

Royal Sonesta This is my choice for the combination of a large hotel (500 units) with the qualities of a French bistro. Outside is wild and crazy Bourbon Street and inside is total tranquility. Ask for an interior room overlooking the garden patio. 300 Bourbon Street (800-343-7170)

Sheraton This is a huge 1200-room hotel on Canal, the main shopping street. I recommend this hotel because of the view from the suites overlooking the Mississippi River. It is magnificent to watch the sunsets or the river traffic early in the morning. A walk across the street puts you back in the French Quarter. 500 Canal Street (504-525-2500 or 800-325-3535)

Hilton Hotel They say that jazz began at the **Pete Fountain Palace** jazz lounge here. I found the best reason to stay at the Hilton is its complete fitness facilities, including an indoor tennis club. The location at Poydras and the Mississippi River is excellent. (800-445-8667)

Bourbon Orleans This small hotel is adjacent to action-packed Bourbon Street, yet it feels intimate and has attractive rooms. 717 Orleans St. (800-521-5338)

If you desire a hotel away from the craziness of Bourbon Street, then try the **Pontchartrain**, an old time grand hotel (800-777-6193) or the **Avenue Plaza Suite Hotel**, which offers apartment-size rooms and a European spa (800-535-9575). Both hotels are in the middle of the peaceful Garden District. Once you're there, you can take the trolley to go back to Bourbon Street area.

In general, hotels like Sheraton, Westin, Marriott, Holiday Inn Crown Plaza, and Hyatt serve primarily business travelers during the week but usually give great discounts on weekends. The quaint, intimate, and unique hotels appeal to a different clientele and often give a better weekday rate than the larger chains. If you make reservations on a toll-free number and the price seems a little high, try calling the hotel direct and you might get a cheaper rate.

Chapter 1

WOMEN AND NIGHTLIFE

There are no curfew laws on liquor in New Orleans, but the club hours vary depending on the party moods of the patrons. Your best bet is simply to follow the crowds on Bourbon Street, and if jazz isn't your thing, then reggae, blues, rock and Cajun music are right around the corner. Walking along Bourbon Street, you will encounter dozens of bars, jazz clubs, restaurants, porno-peek-a-boo houses, topless bars, discos, and whatever else you can think of. As you try out different establishments, your bartender will put your drink in a paper cup so you can ramble with it. Stop when you hear some music that's to your taste or follow the girl in front of you till she picks out a bar, then join her for a drink.

You have heard of the **Hurricane** or **Ramos Gin Fizz** and New Orleans is the inventor. **Pat O'Brien's** (718 St. Peter Street) is probably the most famous bar in America and is certainly worth a stop.

Bourbon Street isn't the only place for nightlife. Go uptown to **Tipitana's** or **Muddy Water** where you'll find the same great music and happy people. A word of caution: as the evening gets going and you decide to barhop around, take a cab. From Bourbon Street to uptown will cost only about $10. Like any metropolitan city, New Orleans has its share of muggers and robbers who get active late at night.

If you can't sleep or just need something to keep you going, head over to the **Cafe du Monde**, open 24 hours in the French Market, for some chicory-flavored coffee mixed with hot milk.

If you think that this entertainment isn't enough, then you should know that riverboat gambling has been recently legalized by the Louisiana state legislature. In late 1993 new paddle boats built for gambling and costing 30 to 40 million dollars each will begin to revitalize the Mississippi River waterfront. They will leave from the waterfront, near the Hilton and Hyatt Regency hotels, and take three-hour cruises up and down the river several times a day. Hilton

Hotels is building a 3,000 passenger riverboat with 1,485 slot machines and 66 gambling tables that will dock in front of its property. It'll soon be Las Vegas in New Orleans.

Finally, you may notice many Japanese tourists milling around New Orleans, one of several American cities (along with Los Angeles and Orlando) which are heavily promoted for tourism in Japan. What you may not know is that the dream of many single Japanese females is to get to know an American; they consider us mysterious. They will not usually look you in the eye or give you an indication that they are interested, but if you approach them cautiously and ask a few simple questions such as what city do they come from or how do they like New Orleans, you might make some new and very interesting friends. Don't let the group mentality bother you; you may actually wind up escorting all of them. The problem is getting one of them away from the group, a fun and challenging task.

TOPLESS NEW ORLEANS

Whether it is Mardi Gras or just mardi (the French word for Tuesday), parties in New Orleans are unmatched anywhere in the United States. I vividly remember one night when I was wandering down Bourbon Street with a drink in hand. It was 11:00 P.M. but the air was still hot and humid. Between two rows of French "maisons," the street was a flowing stream of dancing, yelling, and laughing people. Girls in bustiers and miniskirts danced on the verandas above the crowds, while the people below dared them to pull down their tops or pull up their skirts!

Chapter 1

Eventually the crowd filtered into the shops, discos, and bars. I peered behind a doorway lined with a black stage curtain to discover a live sex show featuring a menage à trois (actually there were five people, to be accurate). I later stepped into a quieter bar, or so I thought. With the dim glow of red light and the whining of the saxophone, a sleazy dancer came out and revealed herself bit by bit. A group of college kids with eyes glued intently on her every wiggle and jiggle were sitting in front of me. She teased them until they couldn't control their claps and cheers. Their table tops became her stage, and then their laps. She ended her act with one lucky guy tucked between her breasts.

With all the peep-shows and topless bars, a lady is not too difficult to find in New Orleans.

GETTING HOME

If you want to save a few dollars, try these bus and limousine companies from your hotel to the airport: **Airport Rhodes** (469-4555) or **Louisiana Transit Co.** (737-9611). Ask at your front desk for schedules, fares, and departure locations.

If you fall in love with the spirit of New Orleans and wonder what it was like a few hundred years ago, then I suggest visiting **Sao Luis**, *a mystical city in northern Brazil. Settled by the French about the same time as New Orleans, this city is steamy, exotic in its music and food, mysterious, and lots of fun. Since there are no direct flights to the city, it can be quite an adventure getting there but the trip is unforgettable. You can read more about Sao Luis in the chapter on Brazil.*

Orlando

You might ask why a single man would want to go to Orlando and Disney World since they are generally considered places for families or couples. But nothing could be further from the truth as I discovered it. They are great places for the single man to recapture the spirit of his boyhood, as well as have some fun.

I went to Orlando because I love science and wanted to see EPCOT Center. When none of my friends would travel with me, I just got on the plane and went. Not only did I have a fantastic time — and meet several new and interesting friends — but I discovered during this trip that traveling alone has its rewards. One advantage is that you do things at your own pace. You don't need to entertain anyone, and you eat and sleep at your leisure. My most important discovery was that I was great company for myself.

I can't guarantee that you fall in love nor have a lusty one-night stand in Orlando, but what you'll find is good old fashioned boyhood fun. Going to EPCOT Center is like walking into a Sharper Image store the size of a Caribbean island, and just one price allows you to try out all the merchandise. You'll be so tired after one day that you can save your romantic notions for better use on a future trip.

GETTING THERE

Orlando's new $300 million airport is a real treat. Other than Singapore and Tampa, no city in the world has a more modern and efficient airport. Not only do elevated trains whisk you to your baggage, but renting a car is a snap and you can be quickly on your way. Most domestic airlines fly to Orlando since it's the vacation and resort capital of the

United States. I suggest flying either Delta because of its ties to Disney World, or United because of its direct service from most cities), or USAir because it seems to have the best prices but not always the most direct route!

Watch out though for package deals that the airlines offer which include hotels. Once you pay, you are stuck at your hotel when you might want to be elsewhere. Remember Murphy's Law: if it's possible to have a family with five teenagers in the room next to you, it will happen. Half of the fun of traveling alone is not being tied to one hotel. Make your reservations yourself, and don't forget to check for off-season discounts. The hotel clerks won't offer them unless you ask, and if one place doesn't suit you, simply move on.

If you've rented a car, leaving the airport is easy. Just get on the Bee Line Expressway and head east until you reach Highway I-4. From there, Orlando is to the north and Disney World to the south. By the way, if you get on the Bee Line Expressway heading west, you'll arrive at the **John F. Kennedy Space Center** in about ninety minutes.

ABOUT THE CITY

If you had a time machine take you back to the early 1950s, you'd see Orlando as just another small, citrus producing, rarely talked about southern town. Then in 1965 Walt Disney purchased 27,000 acres of swampland to the southwest of Orlando and shortly thereafter the new southern style Walt Disney World began. (California's Disney World is only 550 acres vs. a complex of 29,000 acres in Orlando). Between 1970 and 1980 the city population more than doubled and land values rose one thousand percent. In 1983 the new international airport and ultra-modern convention center were finished and Orlando became one of the world's major destinations. The city's nickname is "The City Beautiful".

Orlando is surrounded by low rolling hills covered with orange trees right in the middle of Florida's lake country. There are over 50 lakes around which you can bike, hike or walk and smell the spring blossoms. If you happen to get bored, then head west to Sarasota or Tampa. **Tarpon**

Springs, one of my favorite cities, is only a half hour north of Tampa. Even closer, south of Orlando, is **Cypress Gardens** with its famous water show. To the east is the **John F. Kennedy Space Center** and north of it is the fabled Daytona Beach. If you continue driving north, you'll run into the oldest and one of the most interesting cities in the United States, St. Augustine, founded by Ponce de Leon in 1493 when he sailed with Columbus.

WHERE TO STAY

No other place I can think of has more hotel choices than Orlando; it's simply mind-boggling. First, there are the **Walt Disney Hotels**, which are closest to the main attractions but therefore the most expensive.

Next, there are the hotels of **Lake Buena Vista**, a park-like setting within eye-shot of the Disney lands. If you're trying to cut expenses, then check into a motel on U.S. 192 which intersects I-4. Going left takes you to the motels and right leads to Disney World. This motel row has nearly 50,000 rooms from every motel chain imaginable. A new central reservation office is now open in Kissimee/St. Cloud; calling 800-333-5477 gives you access to 19,000 of these hotel rooms.

A third area of hotels is called **International Drive**, which is about a twenty-minute drive by I-4. This area offers higher quality establishments than motel row, but less expensive than the properties boarding the Disney landscape. A sampling of each area follows:

Dolphin Hotel Managed by Sheraton and possibly the most opulent hotel I've ever seen. With its beach, pools, lakes, huge dolphin statues, futuristic design, and speedboat shuttle to EPCOT Center, this hotel and its sister, the Swan, are Disney at his best. (800-227-1500)

The Contemporary Resort (407-824-1000), with a monorail right through the lobby, and the **Grand Floridia Beach Resort**, (407-824-8000) in the southern architectural style, are just a shade less in price and imagination than the above. Call these Disneyland hotels after 5:00 p.m. EST, when they are less busy, and ask about discount rates.

Hyatt Regency Grand Cypress (800-228-9000) This Lake Buena Vista property is a major attraction for Orlando along with the **Marriott's Orlando World Center** (800-233-1234). Both hotels offer the service of a deluxe chain, but the Marriott is excessively big for my taste, with over 1500 rooms and condos. I prefer the Hyatt, with its eleven-story atrium and rock grotto pool plus a fitness and tennis club.

Orange Lake Country Club If you exit U.S.192 from I-4 and turn left, you enter motel row, but if you turn right towards Disney World, you go onto the Irlo Brownson Memorial Parkway. Keep driving five minutes past the Disney gate, and you'll find this country club with 578 rooms and villas, sixteen tennis courts, a lake for boating or water skiing, an Olympic-size pool, a bowling alley, and a golf course. This is one of the nicer time-share operations

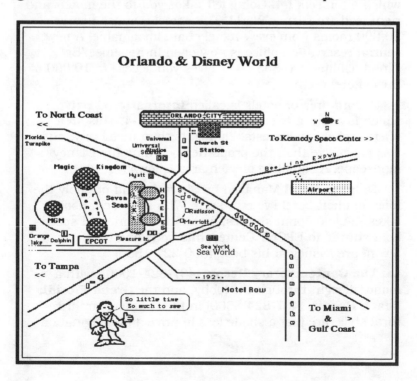

16

and will gladly rent a one- or two-bedroom condo to you with the hope of selling you a time-share. A real bargain for what you get. If you stay a week they will include a free rental car! (407-239-0000 or 800-877-6522)

Radisson Inn & Aquatic Center This property is on International Drive, directly off I-4 a good twenty minutes from Disney World but only a few minutes from Sea World. This area also has hotels from Stouffers, Marriott Inn, Peabody, Hilton Inn, Ramada, Best Western, and so on. The Radisson, however, is my favorite because of its $25-million fitness center with handball and racquetball courts, as well as an Olympic-sized pool with hydraulic roof that opens for high dives. And the rooms are very comfy too; not the Hyatt Regency but half the price. (800-752-0003 or 407-345-0505)

Dixie Landing Resort Walt Disney World has just introduced some budget priced bedrooms. The new Dixie Landing Resort has more than 2,000 rooms and rates start at $85.00 per night. Included is transportation by riverboat to the Disney attractions. (800-647-7900)

WHAT TO DO

Obviously, you're here to go to **Disney World**, but it's a not as easy as one might think. My main complaint is the sheer size; the human body can take only so much walking, noise, traffic, and congestion in one day. There are three main areas: **the Magic Kingdom, Disney MGM Studios, and EPCOT Center.** To do all three would take at least three days of non-stop strolling, leaving little time or energy for other activities. EPCOT Center, so named because it stands for the Experimental Prototype Community of To-morrow, is the main attraction, and the eighth wonder of the world in my estimation.

EPCOT is divided into two sections. **Future World**, where you'll explore such wonders as "Journey into Imagi-nation" - "World of Motion" - "The Land" - "Seabase Alpha" - "The Living Seas" and "Spaceship Earth". After seeing Spaceship Earth, get a map and explore. I found the best plan is to enter the park in the early morning, return to my hotel for a little sun and swim, then go back to EPCOT for dinner and the fireworks and laser show.

The second section of EPCOT, **World Showcase**, a park within itself, contains displays from eleven nations that give you an introduction into foreign cultures. Plan an entire day for this world tour. When you get hungry, the World Showcase has restaurants from all over the world and you can choose from Mexican, French, German, Japanese, Moroccan, Chinese, British, and Swedish foods.

After EPCOT, you can visit the relatively new **MGM Studios**, a short boat trip away, where you can see several live action shows. Stretching out for more than 100 acres, this is one of central Florida's main new attraction. Other than the Hollywood Boulevard art deco shops and restaurants, my favorite exhibit is the Indiana Jones show. A live presentation is given of the movie "Temple of Doom" where the rolling rock almost buries him but he survives miraculously. Of course there is a scary STAR WAR ride, plus all sorts of television, movie, and sound demonstrations. This place is so realistic I felt like I was really in front of the Grauman's Chinese Theater on Hollywood Boulevard.

Third, there's The Magic Kingdom, which is better than Disneyland in California, but not as interesting or as much fun as the one in Tokyo. Personally, I suggest you concentrate on EPCOT if you've been to a Disneyland before. Before attempting The Magic Kingdom, head over to Pleasure Island for some water sports and relaxation. Try renting a miniature power boat for a quick spin around the lake. This is the perfect spot to get away from the crowds and cool down.

While walking around, notice the hoards of Japanese tourists with their cameras. Remember, when you see these groups of girls — actually women, they just look so young — the only person they would rather meet other than Mickey himself is you. Pretend you're lost (an easy thing to happen) and ask for directions. There is always one who can speak a little English and can't wait to try. Join the group and let them take you to a Japanese restaurant. Don't be embarrassed when they try to pay for you; it's their custom to treat guests. This strategy has never failed me.

Another way of meeting women in Disney World, a mecca of single (divorced) moms vacationing with their children, is to help a worn-out mother who would love the helpful companionship of an altruistic and understanding male. Just make sure the kid is to your liking, for if Murphy's law works you'll wind up spending more time with him (her) than the mom.

In addition to the Disney complexes, there are many more interesting sites and attractions. The most publicized is **Universal Studios**, but I found this to be a major disappointment because the environment is fake and nothing worked. In fact, so many things were inoperable the day I was there that they gave me not one, but two free return vouchers.

*Disney also considered the adult and built a special place. At the far end of the footbridge over Buena Vista Lagoon is **Pleasure Island,** a good reason to stay at the Disney Village Hotel Plaza with its half-dozen or so hotels. Not only is this a 'R' rated area — no one under 18 can be admitted without an adult — but this complex contains 6 nightclubs, 4 restaurants, and shops and movie theaters. You'll get heavy metal sounds at "The Cage", country music at the "Neon Armadillo Music Saloon", oldies at the "XZFR Rock & Roll Beach Club", and a comedy club adjacent to a mystic magical emporium called the "Adventure Club." The bars really don't start till after 7.00 P.M. and the disco after 9.00 P.M. With all its hedonistic activities, a sort of Disney Yuppie Land, it's a good place to go if you are into the mingling mood and don't feel like driving back to Orlando. If you have any lustful thoughts, wander over to "Jessica's " to check out the latest in see-through red lingerie. If you still have energy left, try one of the five golf courses, for a total of 99 holes! Some people call Disney World the "Magic Linkdom."*

Chapter 2

In Orlando, for a great night out on the town, **Church Street Station** is the place to be. It's in Orlando proper; go north on I-4, then follow the signs. This old railroad depot is a major attraction with funky songs, dancing, saloons, can-can girls, restaurants, and an atmosphere of total fun. Don't miss **Rosie O'Grady's Good Time Emporium**.

SIDETRIPS OUT OF TOWN

Heading out the other direction on the Bee Line Expressway, is the **John F. Kennedy Space Center**. Here you might be lucky enough to see the Space Shuttle getting ready. There is a NASA escorted bus tour that includes a glimpse of real moon rocks.

A few hours' drive west on I-4 takes you to Tampa and **Bush Gardens**. Here you'll find the Dark Continent, an authentic turn-of-the-century Africa with all the wild animals, gardens, rides, flowers, and shops you could imagine.

If you are a hotel buff as I am, none has more grandeur than the **Don CeSar Hotel** at 3400 Gulf Boulevard in St. Petersburg Beach, a thirty-minute drive over the long spanning bridges from Tampa. This hotel was built in 1928 by a land-boom Floridian millionaire who thought that pink was in! The hotel has been totally restored and is on the National Register of Historical Places. The restoration included an expansion of the beach and water sports facilities, an Olympic pool, a tennis club, 13,900 panes of glass, original Austrian crystal chandeliers, and all exterior walls repainted in Don CeSar rouge. As you approach the hotel over the bridge, you'll see a huge pink mirage and you know you've arrived. If you check in, you might be staying in the same room that F. Scott Fitzgerald, Babe Ruth, Lou Gehrig, or Clarence Darrow played and slept in. (800-247-9810)

If you make it to Sarasota, the new cultural capital of Florida that also has a nice beach, great art galleries, concerts, operas and the Ringling estate full of original circus artifacts, I suggest you stay at the **Colony Beach Resort**. With 232 suites and 21 tennis courts it is a sportsman's paradise. (800-237-9443)

Less than a hour north of Tampa, on the Gulf of Mexico, is Tarpon Springs. This village, a few miles from the great beaches of Clearwater on US 19A, is the perfect getaway beach resort with a relaxing Greek village heritage. Here live the descendants of Greek fisherman among mansions and bayous. If a feta salad is to your liking or your sweet tooth craves some Baklava, then regroup from Disney World here. The best place to stay is the **Innisbrook Resort**, only ten minutes away and famous for its superb golf course and restaurants. (800-456-2000)

The ultimate sports getaway is the **Saddlebrook Golf and Tennis Resort**. Only 25 miles from the Tampa airport, this resort offers 37 hard and clay tennis courts plus full golf and spa facilities. (800-237-7519)

GETTING HOME

Since Orlando is the rent-a-car capital of the world, your car return will be effortless. As you arrive at the airport, your agency will have a flag-man showing you where to park and another agent will complete the bill on the spot. A porter is standing by to carry all your purchases and gifts.

Don't forget to reconfirm your return flight home, as this is one busy airport. Alternatively, buy an open-jaws ticket from your departure city that allows you to leave from a different city than the one you arrived in. These tickets usually don't cost more and give you some flexibilty. After a brief stay in Tampa or St. Petersberg as suggested, you can return your car at the Tampa airport and leave from there, making a return to Orlando unnecessary.

Palm Springs

Palm Springs has been one of my favorite vacation areas for the last thirty years. When I was in college, this was the place to go in the search for that perfect female body. During my early- and mid-twenties, it was Yuppie heaven, the place to be seen. Now it's my favorite place just to kick back, take a walk or hike, and spoil myself with lush accommodations. If you've never walked in the desert evening, seen every star imaginable, felt the desert wind, and eaten ice cream on Palm Canyon Boulevard as fabulous miniskirted women walk by, then you're in for the treat of a lifetime.

The Palm Springs area also includes the entire Coachella Valley, a never-ending series of small towns, each with its unique resorts, restaurants, and activities. The most popular are: **Palm Desert**, with its mega-resorts and shopping center; **Indian Wells**, which has become the new in place; **La Quinta**, with the most famous and lush resort in the area; and **Rancho Mirage**, with its famous restaurant row. Close by are also **Indio**, with its date farms, and **Desert Hot Springs**, with its bubbling hot mineral water baths to soothe your pains.

With over seventy courses in the vicinity, Palm Springs has been called the golf capital of the world. There are also more than 7,000 swimming pools and over 600 tennis courts. You can hike in the San Jacinto mountains, bike through the cities, enjoy the view from an aerial tramway or from balloon flights, or stroll through a huge water park with multiple slides. This is definitely the place for the single male to explore.

CLIMATE

Palm Springs averages 88 degrees Fahrenheit during the day, 55 degrees at night, although in the height of the summer it can get to 115 degrees during the day. The best time to visit is just off-season in May and June or September and October when it's hot enough to keep the crowds

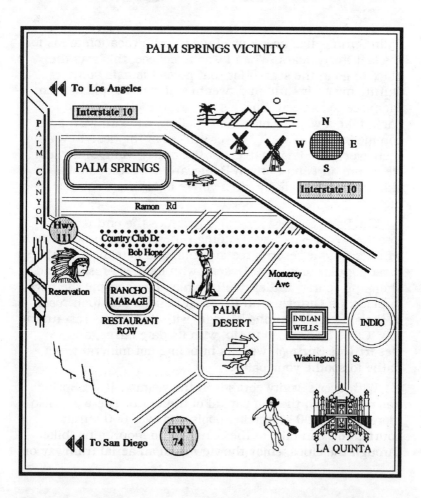

PALM SPRINGS VICINITY

away and the tanned bikini-minded are still there. Average low (night) and high (day) temperatures for some typical months are as follows:

February	43 - 72	September	66 - 102
May	57 - 94	October	57 - 91
June	64 - 102	December	41 - 70

The high temperatures may seem a little scary, but there is no humidity, so spending the day poolside surrounded by beautiful women couldn't be better. If you want to jog or play tennis, it's better to do so in the early mornings or late afternoons. There's also plenty of early evening happy hours at restaurants and cafes, and they are crowded with people trying to cool off.

GETTING THERE

The Palm Springs airport, at the end of Tahquitz Boulevard (the main east-west thoroughfare in Palm Springs) was a gift from Pearl McCallum McManus and was designed by the famous Mexican architect Julio de la Pena. I like the airport for its proximity to the hotels and its central location in the Coachella Valley, not to mention its beautiful fountains! It's worth it to rent a car and you'll find the usual national firms plus Ajax (619-320-7441) and Select (619-320-5781).

The airport handles American (with service to Dallas and Chicago), Delta (with service to Salt Lake City), TWA (with service to St. Louis), United (with service to San Francisco and Denver), U.S. Air (with a new service to Los Angeles), American West (with service to Las Vegas and Phoenix), and the local carrier Skywest. All have direct or connecting flights, and some have non-stop but shop carefully as the most direct are usually the most expensive. A new carrier to Palm Springs is Alaska Airlines (with service to Portland and Seattle), which is rated as one of the best airlines in the world for food and service.

As I suggested for your trip to Orlando, an open-jaws ticket is very useful to get in some extra sightseeing in California. For example, you might land in Palm Springs, rent a car, and then return from any of the airports in the southern California area (including LAX, Ontario, Burbank, Long Beach, San Diego, or even John Wayne in the Newport Beach area).

The Palm Springs airport is within walking distance of one of my favorite hotels, the Wyndham with its enormous pool, so you can rent a car at your leisure. Note though that renting at a local rent-a-car, rather than at the airport, is cheaper but will not allow you to return the car at another airport. A national chain like Avis allows free drop-offs. A word to the wise: always reconfirm the free drop-offs at different airports because hidden rental car expense surprises are a common occurrence! Many of my best trips have ended with long, heated, and losing arguments at the rental counter.

WHERE TO STAY

The Palm Springs area offers so many choices that it's really a question of your preferences and pocketbook.

I suggest starting off in Palm Springs proper to get the feel of the city and the desert, then move to another area of the valley if Palm Springs is not your style or if curiosity simply gets the best of you. Call 800-34-SPRINGS for a free 32-page vacation guide. In the meantime, here's a list of my recommended hotels:

Wyndham Close to the airport and the center of the town, with a fantastic pool. Popular on weekends with many Los Angeles area sun seekers, including some beautiful women wearing string bikinis. The pool does get a little oily from the large crowds. The Wyndham is my choice if you like a crowd to socialize with. Ask for a mini-suite facing the pool and the the discount weekend package, if available. (800-822-4200)

Palm Springs Hilton A block closer to town than the Wyndham, this former Plaza and Sheraton is a beautiful hotel with its own tennis club across the street. (619-320-6868)

Marquis Hotel Across the street from the Hilton and the adjoining new mall with a multiple movie theater. The annex portion offers the best value in suites. (619-322-2121 or 800-223-1050)

Palm Springs Riviera The former Radisson, this hotel is now completely remodeled and is an outstanding resort. Mayor Sonny Bono's restaurant and racquet club are adjacent to the hotel. The Riviera has one of the largest swimming pools in Palm Springs. The only drawback is that it is not within walking distance of the main shopping district and entertainment area. (619-327-8311)

Hyatt Regency Suites This is the old Maxim's hotel, elegant in every way. The lobby is breathtaking and is connected to the Desert Plaza Mall so you never have to leave air-conditioned comfort to shop, sleep, and eat. The problem is that the pool is small and poorly designed, although the surroundings are lush. (619-322-9000)

Oasis Water Villa Hotel This is a condo development that didn't sell and so was turned into a hotel. It's a little out of town, but worth the drive, as you get not only a fully

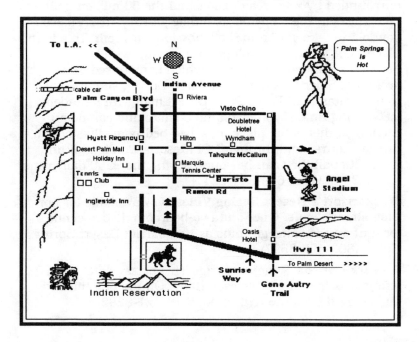

furnished condo but eight pools, racquetball courts, tennis club, full spa privileges and free passes to the water park. (800-543-5160 or 619-328-1499)

The Tennis Club This is a time-share arrangement, but one that allows vacationers to rent the condos. Formerly one of the great places to stay, all rooms are suites or larger. It has the most photogenic pool in Palm Springs, and you can take one of their bikes or walk to town. A bonus is the best tennis club in town with a convenient matchmaker. (619-325-1441)

Four Seasons Across the street from the Tennis Club and every bit as nice. If your taste is small, cozy, and private, this is the place. The pool is nice and the rooms and suites are extremely clean. If you play tennis, ask Hal for a membership to the Tennis Club during your stay; you play as his guest. (619-325-6427)

Marriott's Desert Springs Resort This is the yuppie resort of the desert. A true mega-resort with fourteen lakes, two golf courses, ten restaurants, a luxury spa, and a private beach, all on four hundred acres. This property is surrounded by 23 acres of lakes and the 50 million-gallon lake starts in the lobby on its 3 mile journey. There's even a gondola to take you from the lobby to your room. This is the place to be seen, but don't get it mixed up with the Marriott's Rancho Las Palmas, which is more sedate and secluded. Since this hotel is in Palm Desert, you are close to the fantastic El Paseo Palm Desert mall with its indoor ice-skating rink. If you own a time-share and can do an exchange, this is the place; new two-bedroom villas adjoin the golf course and through RCI (Resorts Condominium International) they can be yours, saving the $250 daily rate. (800-228-9290 or 619-341-2211)

Marriott's Desert Spring Villas Now available for non time-share clients. One- and two-bedroom deluxe condo's for rent on the same grounds as the Marriot Desert Springs Hotel. (800-526-3597)

Ritz-Carlton Rancho Mirage This classy hotel has 10 tennis courts and marble everything. On top of a hill and far removed from the real world. (619-321-8282)

The Tennis Club Pool

Stouffer Esmeralda Resort In Indian Wells across from the Hyatt Grand Champions Resort (which has a 10,500-seat tennis stadium and 24 pools). The Esmeralda is a 560-room wonderland with a Ted Robinson-designed 36-hole golf course. (619-773-4444)

La Quinta Hotel For the hotel buff, this is it. Located 19 miles southeast of Palm Springs, past Palm Desert but close to Indio. An acclaimed hotel since 1926, it has exquisite rooms and suites, its own shopping complex, nine pools and spas, free bicycles, a Pete Dye-designed golf course on the premises and 30 tennis courts (6 grass, 3 clay). There are wonderful early morning views of the mountains, but my favorite experience is when the staff brings you break-fast on tricycles. You can hike the Santa Rosa mountains. A new $50 million renovation has made this hotel very, very special. (800-854-1271 or 619-564-4111)

Sunrise Rentals This company handles five of the most prestigious country clubs and helps you to rent someone's fully-furnished condo. My favorite is Palm Valley; it has many social activities, a complete, self-contained fitness club and is close to Palm Desert entertainment. (800-869-1130 or 619-345-5695)

Chapter 3

Lawrence Welk Resort I include this desert oasis because it's the steal of the desert. Simply call up and say you are interested in a time-share and they will book a four-day, three-night package during mid-week or a two-night Friday and Saturday stay for under $100.00! You get a villa, free tennis, an activity center, and half-price golf fees. It's only minutes from downtown Palm Springs. The catch, of course, is that you must attend a ninety-minute sales pitch, but you don't need to buy. This is a beautiful property. (800-676-0002 Ext. 1218)

Marriott time-share has a similar offer but a little more expensive and restrictive on days available. (800-235-6618)

In addition to the above time-shares, another choice would be Desert Breezes Time Share in South Palm Desert. This 75-acre oasis sits between Palm Desert and the La Quinta area and has all the amenities. (619- 345-2637)

Time-Share: Scam or Great Deal: If you've never considered time-share condos, here's the scoop. Personally, I feel the purchase of weekly condominiums is wasteful. On the other hand, purchasing these units second-hand at 50% discounts has often provided me with comfortable surroundings on my travels. A condo with all the amenities is certainly better than an over-priced hotel room. I have spent serene nights in Aruba, Cancun, the Bahamas, Mazatlan, Hawaii, and Palm Springs in time-share condominiums. The trick is to buy them used and then exchange wisely from time to time to another location. If you can choose your vacation time, you can beat the system by using the instant exchange provision which allows you to upgrade to any available unit. For instance, I recently traded a two-year old one-bedroom for a three-bedroom villa in Mexico. However, always say there are six people in your party even if you are going solo. These bargains can be found in the classifieds in large circulation newspapers, especially in USA Today. Concentrate on purchasing a two-bedroom, high-season unit, as you can exchange more easily if you can't pick your vacation time. Once you have purchased one, test it out.

Both Palm Springs and Puerto Vallarta have abundant selections. When it comes to exchanging, I suggest that you research the units the trading company wants you to exchange for. Ask questions and get the phone numbers of people who've been there! They often try to unload the most unpopular units first, such as those furthest from the water or overlooking the parking lot.

Another useful point is not to exchange for a place like Orlando because there's no reason to waste an expensive time-share week in an area of abundant good cheap rooms. In Florida there are so many rooms available that it's a waste to use up your exchange week. People forget that the yearly maintenance fee plus property taxes can add up to about $350-$500. This is another factor in the equation of figuring out if a time-share is for you, even if you can purchase it at a 50 percent discount. If you are considering a foreign time-share, you have the advantage of not paying taxes but your unit usually doesn't exchange as easily as a unit in the United States. And this is important for you too, as when your unit is taken in exchange, your own priority increases dramatically when you request an exchange.

WHAT TO DO

I return every month or so to the desert because I never get tired of it. You can either take advantage of all that there is to do, or you do nothing but relax by the pool if you so desire.

I do suggest taking the **Aerial Tramway** in Palm Springs. This gondola-like car takes you up 8,516 feet to 54 miles of hiking or viewing trails. This is probably the only place in the world where you go from 110 degrees at the bottom to fluffy white snow in five minutes as you arrive at the top of the mountains. If you prefer hiking, my favorite trail starts at the end of Ramon Road and climbs over the Tennis Club until all of Palm Springs is in view. On your way down Ramon, toward Palm Canyon Boulevard, stop off at the **Ingleside Inn** to have a drink and fantasize what Katharine Hepburn and Spencer Tracy might have said to each other while drinking there.

Chapter 3

There are also balloon flights, marked bicycle trails, a 75,000-square-foot desert museum featuring native American sculpture and painting (located behind Fashion Plaza mall), an ultra-modern water park with a "beach and waves" called **Oasis Waterpark**, a living desert exhibition which combines desert wildlife and a botanical park inside a 1200 acre expanse, and horseback riding through the Indian Reservations. One of the more unusual sights is the **Salton Sea**. North of Brawley, the sea is 38 miles long and 228 feet below sea level. Mud puddles at the far tip are believed to lie directly over the San Andreas Fault. If you can't swim this is your place since you can't sink in the Salton Sea. Visiting this attraction gives you an idea what the Dead Sea in Israel is like.

If your hotel doesn't have tennis courts, try the **Tennis Center** at 1300 Baristo Road. Not only are there teaching pro's, ball-machines, and tournaments but they will find a game for you (320-0020). If your hotel's pool isn't up to your expectations, try the **Palm Springs Swim Center** in Sunrise Park at the intersection of Sunrise Way and Ramon; the Los Angeles Angels have their spring training here during the summer. The pool features a 50-meter Olympic-size public pool with restricted hours for lap swimmers, and it has a spacious lawn and sun deck. This is a great place to meet locals or just to get away from the screaming kids at a hotel pool.

Besides the guided balloon flights over the desert floor there are some interesting tours: Gray Line Tours has a celebrity tour daily (325-0974), Palm Springs Safari has desert tours that include wineries and landmarks (320-4664), Canyon Adventures has a four-hour fishing trip to White Water Canyon (328-3786), and perhaps the most fun is the Wilderness Jeep Tour that takes you through the rugged desert to an oases (324-3378).

If you are a shopper, the entire Palm Springs vicinity is world-renowned for designer clothes, art work, and interesting nicknacks. The best places are the Desert Fashion Plaza adjacent to the Hyatt Regency Hotel, or Palm Canyon Drive and the famous El Paseo (Palm Desert's equivalent to Rodeo Drive) in Palm Desert. A special treat is the Palm Desert

Town Center Mall that has 150 stores and an ice skating ring to cool down on. This is also a good place to see what the desert women wear to stay cool and it sure does turn up the heat. This is a fun place to stroll, eat, flirt and even dance.

In the long run though, my favorite activity is just an evening stroll down Palm Canyon Boulevard in 80-degree temperatures. Walking, browsing, and flirting is the way of life in this resort city. While it's an unusual practice in the United States, it makes you feel like you are in South America or Asia. What a great way to enjoy a balmy evening!

A new street fair has begun every Thursday night from 6:30 to 9:30 p.m. To attract tourists, Palm Springs now closes Palm Canyon Boulevard and makes it a pedestrian way. There are bands, strolling performers, handcrafts, food and a certified farmer's market. A enjoyable way to spend a desert evening.

If all this is not enough, head out towards San Bernardino via Highway 18 until the Lake Arrowhead cut-off and in about an hour and a half you'll be viewing Lake Arrowhead, one of the prettiest lakes in California. Here you'll find 60 shops, boutiques, restaurants overlooking the lake, and a great Hilton Hotel, with condo rooms to rent. There's also lake boats, tennis courts, a pool, and an aerobics center. 714-336-1511.

SPORTING EVENTS

For sport nuts, go to the Bob Hope Classic, the Nabisco Dinah Shores LPGA, the Vintage Arco Invitional and the Frank Sinatra Celebritiy golf championships. For tennis buffs, there is the Newsweek Champions Cup in Indian Wells and the Virginia Slim in Palm Springs. Contact the Chamber of Commerce for exact dates. (619-325-1577)

Chapter 3

Warning: I've passed out twice in my life, both times in Palm Springs. The first time was while playing tennis during mid-day; the second time was in a fancy restaurant after a day of sports, drinking, and afternoon carousing - I was carried back to my hotel on a stretcher! Remember, the desert is low humidity ... perspiration quickly evaporates, and you might not be aware of the sun's strength, so don't be fooled. To prevent heat exhaustion, wear a hat, drink lots of water rather than alcohol, eat lightly, and avoid high-noon activities (unless you're in an air-conditioned room!).

WOMEN AND NIGHTLIFE

Probably the best bar to watch women in Palm Springs is at the **Las Casuelas Mexican restaurant**. Note that there are two restaurants by this name in Palm Springs; make sure you wind up at the one on South Palm Canyon called "Teraza." The food is overrated, but for a good reason even during mid-week summer the place is packed. The bar is a great place to make new friends while waiting for dinner. Ask for patio seating to watch the strollers in bikini tops.

Speaking of food, I must digress here to recommend two of my favorite restaurants that make a trip to Palm Springs worth the drive. First, **Louise's Pantry** (on Palm Canyon Blvd. just before Tahquitz McCallum going north) is excellent for its home-cooked meals and pies. **Nate's Delicatessen** (100 S. Indian Avenue) has been there for over 40 years and is world renowned as Mr. Corned Beef.

Another great place to people-watch and have a light meal is **Brussels Cafe**, on Palm Canyon Boulevard. The setting is perfect to watch the parade of women, and the food is priced reasonably. On weekends, they have a jazz and comedy club inside. The strawberry waffles are perfect for that light meal before a night out on the town.

The recently-opened **Cafe Cabo Grill and Cantina** has become the new people-watching bar. Located on Tahquitz Canyon a block from Palm Canyon Boulevard, you can choose the inside restaurant or you can lounge in the patio which includes an exciting sports bar with free tacos during Happy Hour.

Desert View

During the day the Holiday Inn has a new mist-cooling system where one can lay in the sun yet be cooled by a fine water spray. Go have lunch, watch people by the pool and stay cool!

Another possibility in Palm Springs is the refurbished Hamburger Hamlet on Palm Canyon Boulevard, which offers every kind of burger conceivable and a cafe patio where you can sit back, have a drink, and flirt with your neighbors.

There's a great restaurant row in Rancho Mirage as you drive towards Palm Desert. Here you will find La Cave, Medium Rare, Charley Brown's, The Beach House, Kobe Steak House, and Black Angus (good for dancing). My favorite, a few miles down Highway 111 on Bob Hope Drive, is Dar Maghreb, a Moroccan restaurant where you sit on the floor and eat with your fingers while a belly-dancer performs for you.

Chapter 3

Dancing and Clubs

A VERY COOL BAR AND GRILLE
SPECIALIZING IN FROZEN DRINKS

If you like dancing and gazing, Palm Springs has its share of clubs. For the young at heart, there is **Zelda's**, across the street from the Spa Hotel on Indian Avenue. If you want to join the action, try **Chiller's.** The newest disco/bar/live music and mingling center of Palm Springs, it is located on Palm Canyon Boulevard adjacent to Las Casuelas restaurant. This is the Hot Spot, three levels of bars, and the drinks are premixed and stored in hanging vats, and four patios to dance and flirt by. This is my favorite spot. There's no need to dress up, and be prepared for all sorts of women. The night I was there, a Los Angeles fashion model group, a women's business group, plus locals from the community were all circulating the bars checking out the guys.

For sophistication, try **Cecil's** at 1775 E. Palm Canyon Blvd. in the Smoke Tree Shopping Center. Another popular spot is **Pompeii**, a fifteen-minute drive out towards Cathedral City, although this restaurant and disco is a little too garish for my taste with the stereotypical Mr. Muscles in the parking lot who screens you before you enter. If you like to dance but Disco isn't your style, then try **Hank's Fish House and Night Club** in the newly renovated Holiday Inn. Besides a great restaurant, the music is geared to the over 30's clientele and the bar is very friendly.

For mellow hotel lounge entertainment, try the Wyndham Hotel or across the street, the Hilton. The best hotel bar is in the Riviera Hotel. If you are a night owl and still have energy left, then try **Mary's**, next to Bono's restaurant, at 1700 North Indian Avenue. This is a late-night disco for the more sophisticated browser. Who knows, maybe Sonny might drop in!

For a quiet piano bar, the best is **Melvyn's at the Ingleside Inn**, the finest restaurant in Palm Springs, located at 200 W. Ramon Road, one block toward the mountains from Palm Canyon.

In Palm Desert, you'll find the crowd to be a little older, not as fast paced, but just as fun. Take Highway 111, the road leading out of Palm Springs, but watch out for traffic during dinner time and early evening. On weekends, the trip to El Paseo in Palm Desert can take 45 minutes or more instead of the usual 20 minutes. If you like the Palm Desert area better, change hotels as there are always rooms available due to the overbuilding of hotels in the valley.

In Palm Desert proper, the place to be is the **Red Onion** restaurant in the El Paseo shopping center, where you can watch the ice-skaters from your table during Happy Hour and eat enough appetizers to skip dinner. If this is not to your taste, across the street is **T.G.I.F.**, which has a busy but noisy bar. Across the way is El Paseo Drive for outdoor shopping and browsing.

Meeting Women Through High Technology

There is a new system in meeting women in the United States. A few years ago match-maker ads were the rage: you wrote an ad, paid to have it published and hoped that a nice girl would respond. Or perhaps you responded to a woman's ad in the personals columns of your local newspaper. Today technology has taken over and instead of waiting a week for a response, you now can do it in a few hours! Palm Springs is the perfect place to try this technology. Here you have lots of leisure time and probably a strong desire for a companion to show you the sights. Voice-Mail Introduction service is not only fun but very fast. It works by placing an ad in the local paper, and then recording your personal greeting on a voice mail phone number. People responding to your ad can instantaneously leave a response on the phone for you. Have your ad placed before your arrival by calling 800-765-3283 to put your telephone ad in the Palm Springs Desert Sun. The Friday edition has fifty personal ads and they also have a Sports Network telephone column; this is handy if you prefer a sports date rather than a dinner date.

Or you can browse through the women's recorded ads on the telephone for a per minute charge. Then just pick one out, leave a message explaining your interests and cross your fingers for your lucky day. You will have to pay a

few dollars for the 900 service but it certainly adds a little
mystery to your trip. Women are curious beings and check
their voice mail almost every day. What a great way to get
an instant date. Of course you also run the risk of getting
an overweight, self-centered, yappity smoker but life is a
gamble and you won't know till you try.

ADDITIONAL ATTRACTIONS

Besides the beautiful weather, bikini-clad women,
designer shops, great hotels, picturesque surroundings,
and sports galore there are a few surprises that make the
Palm Springs area a great travel experience.

The **Indian Canyons,** ancestral home of the Agua
Caliente band of Cahuilla Indians, is the largest natural
palm oasis in North America. Here are countless
Washingtonia filifera palms, the only palms native to this
continent, growing along the streams, a beautiful and lush
sight in the middle of the desert.

Then there are the dates, the kind you eat. About 99
percent of America's dates are grown in the Coachella
Valley, which has 250,000 date-producing palms. There are
over one hundred varieties of dates grown and many date
stores dot the road to Indio. An enjoyable way to spend an
afternoon is to go out to these roadside markets and try the
varieties of unknown dates. My favorite is Hadleys on
Interstate 10, on the way back to Los Angeles.

A few hours away from Palm Springs is the town of
Temecula. Once a famous stagecoach stop and an historical western town, today it still has an old-time Main Street,
antique shops, and an Old Temecula Museum. For a treat,
go out to the dozen local wineries that surround the area,
nearly all with free tasting rooms.

My favorite oddity is the **San Gorgonio Pass** where
there are are more than 4000 wind turbines lined up,
producing enough electricity for 93,000 homes in southern
California. Driving through this barren, sparse, and rocky
area makes you feel as if you have landed on a Martian
desert.

GETTING HOME

A word of warning: if you plan to drive to LAX for a flight, take at least an extra hour to get there. If you plan to stop in downtown Los Angeles or the valley, remember that they are building the new metro-rail downtown and also the overcrowded and deteriorating Ventura 101 freeway. Expect long delays. Good luck.

From the Palm Springs airport, work is continuing on the first phase of a multimillion-dollar expansion and remodeling project. The five-year plan includes a second runway, a new terminal, and baggage-claim expansion. Also the number of gates will be increased from 8 to 11. The airport is a breeze and the first phase of expansion is already completed.

FINAL NOTES *Palm Springs grows on you. Perhaps it's the calm, the beauty, or the dry heat. Maybe it's simply that the desert fits your moods. You'll discover small quaint hideaways for that "I want to get lost and nobody's going to find me" mood. Or you can find those elegant glass-enclosed marbled hotels for that "let's make new friends" mood. There is nothing like a desert evening or the morning dew at sunrise. Yes, this is a magical place.*

Puerto Vallarta

Going to Mexico twenty years ago was an exotic and adventurous journey; today it's just a simple airplane flight. Yet in many ways such a trip is perfect for the single male to gain confidence and prepare himself for traveling alone to more remote places.

Being in Mexico is extremely different from being in the United States: the poverty, the hassles, the slow service, the water that you must not drink, the "manana" attitude towards business meetings and appointments of any kind, the women that are never on time, and the entire culture that is hard to understand but so beautiful to watch. Being in Mexico also means sharing the beach, restaurants, night clubs, taxis, and hotels with many other Americans or Canadians. You get pestered by time-share salesmen. Beach vendors and taxi drivers double their rates because you are a tourist. What we hear about foreigners who dislike us from television images and gossip is true in Mexico.

But this is your chance to show patience and grace, rather than an ugly-American image. Accept being a peso man and have fun. Meet some of those Mexicans on the beach; they do love to practice their English and most want to visit the United States. You will perhaps make new friends, but most likely they will be Canadians.

Chapter 4

As for the best resort in Mexico, Puerto Vallarta is my choice, and that is what this chapter is about. Here you will find great beaches, cobblestone streets, red-tile roofs, a variety of activities such as hiking, island hopping, tennis, and sight-seeing, as well as excellent seafood restaurants, many moderately-priced hotels, and a clean and beautiful Malecon (boardwalk) where you can walk and browse to your heart's content.

Another advantage of Puerto Vallarta is its proximity to Guadalajara, only half an hour by air. The middle-class, working girls of Guadalajara often make Puerto Vallarta their vacation spot. What an opportunity for you to meet exciting, beautiful women. Remember, however, that this is a strict Catholic country, and flirting and romance take on new meaning. Patience is a must. (Don't worry, we'll soon be in countries where you can throw patience out the window.)

GETTING THERE

Puerto Vallarta is one of the most charming of Mexico's cities, and it's easy to get there, unpack, and be on the beach all in one day. In addition to the Mexican airlines Mexicana and Aeromexico, three main U.S. airlines make the trip: Delta, American, and Continental. Alaska Airlines is another possibility and offers great prices and service, especially if you connect through a west-coast hub. Their flights alternate LAX-Mazatlan-Puerto Vallarta and return non-stop to LAX. The next day the schedule is reversed. The advantage to using the Mexican carriers is that they are usually cheaper and offer more non-stop flights. It used to be that for every American flight to Mexico, a Mexican flight would have to go to the United States. Now, however, Mexico is desperate for more tourists and has opened up its airways for more American flights. Look for new promotional fares.

Aeromexico (800-237-6639) has an inexpensive upgrade to first class program, especially from East Coast cities. Another suggestion is that if you must fly into Mexico with a connection, try Guadalajara instead of Mexico City airport, which is very confusing. If you've never been to Mexico before and would like to see more, then ask to fly Mexicana Airlines, since they usually allow a free stop-over on international routes, which can be very handy for seeing several cities for the price of one.

Of course, the American airlines are more punctual, offer better food, and use newer equipment. Once on a Mexicana flight to Puerto Vallarta from Los Angeles, we stopped in Mazatlan and the new pilot forgot to show up. The Mexican airlines have gotten better, however, due to increased competition, but if you are the demanding type, fly American.

ABOUT THE CITY

Puerto Vallarta is a relatively new resort; regular flights into Puerto Vallarta did not begin until 1954. It wasn't until 1963 with the release of **Night of the Iguana**, directed by John Huston and starring Richard Burton and Ava Gardner that this isolated beach resort achieved notoriety. The scandal of Elizabeth Taylor shacking up with Burton in this Catholic country certainly helped the promotion.

Puerto Vallarta is in one of the most interesting regions of Mexico. The state of Jalisco is famous for mariachi bands, tequila, sangria (the red mixer for our favorite drink: the margarita), and the charros (the famous Mexican cowboy). Unlike other modern beach resorts, the city of Puerto Vallarta had a separate hotel-zone development, allowing it to retain its original style. The charm of the cobblestone streets, red-tile roofs, palm trees, brightly colored flowers and of course the majestic boardwalk makes this my favorite resort of Mexico.

Puerto Vallarta's river, the Cuale, divides the city into northern and southern sections. About two-thirds of the city is on the northern side, including the airport, hotel row, and most of the commerce. The southern end is more residential and calm, especially Playa Los Muertos, and here is where you'll find the old-time bars and discos. At the southern end is the famous Camino Real, the most elegant hotel chain in Mexico, comparable to our Hyatt Regency Hotels, and a beautiful bar for sunset-watching, the Lobby Bar.

43

Chapter 4

A number of Americans have retired in the southern part of town and have made their home in Gringo Gulch, the area above the river. With the inexpensive housing, beautiful people, lush forests and tropical climate, it's hard to believe that you are only a few hours flying time away from Los Angeles. Don't assume you'll be the only tourist. Today about 1.5 million vacationers pass through the city's 10,000 hotel rooms each year. Thanks to the 25 miles of fine beaches (two only reached by boat - La Animas and Yelpa) and no large hotels in the city center, Puerto Vallarta retains its colonial charm and one never feels overwhelmed by the tourists.

CLIMATE

A word of warning: from late June to early October it can be very wet and humid. If you go after Easter or before Christmas, you may need a jacket or a sweater. The best time to travel is after Easter vacation or before the Christmas season.

WHERE TO STAY

One of the advantages of Puerto Vallarta is that the airport is almost in the center of town. A second advantage for the traveller is the abundance of great hotels. From the airport, hotel row is just a few miles or about a five-minute ride in a Volkswagen mini-bus, usually with no air-conditioning. There are no taxis at the airport, but on your return you can take a private taxi. If you are in a hurry, you can rent the entire bus for about $10 and not worry about being accommodating to others. Remember, you are in Mexico, and sometimes things just don't make sense.

From hotel row (Los Tules beach) it's about two miles south to town. The Rio Cuale river dissects the town, with the cheaper hotel area farther south at Playa Los Muertos, a great beach for meeting Mexican ladies and just wandering around. Back to hotel row and going north is the Marina, where the cruise ships dock. Past the marina is the new development area of exotic hotels. Since the airport is situated between hotel row and the new Marina Vallarta area, I recommend the following (traveling north to south):

Marina Beach Area

A mile north of the airport, this brand-new area now includes six resorts with the world-renown Ritz Carlton and Conrad Hotels opening in late 1992. This is the largest, privately-financed tourism project in Mexico, and by the end of the decade, when work on this 450-acre project is completed, there will be 12,000 hotel units. The resorts are being built around Mexico's largest marina and will include a 210-store shopping mall, an office park, condominiums, homes and apartments.

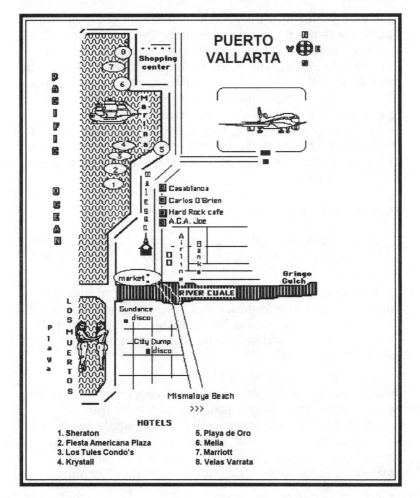

HOTELS

1. Sheraton	5. Playa de Oro
2. Fiesta Americana Plaza	6. Melia
3. Los Tules Condo's	7. Marriott
4. Krystall	8. Velas Varrata

Marriott Casa Magna Resort A brand new hotel in the Marina area. Huge pool shaped like a giant cloverleaf with one leaf touching the ocean. Behind this pool is a swan lake. The only negative is a poor beach. (800-228-9290)

Melia Puerto Vallarta Located next to the Marriott, this may be the most interesting new hotel in Mexico. Melia is the Spanish hotel chain, with its head office in Madrid. This hotel is only a half-mile from the airport, and with 406 rooms and a lake for a pool you can't go wrong. The Melia combines European flair with a Mexican atmosphere. (800-336-3542)

Velas Vallarta In the American tradition of an all-suites hotel, this is the newest and certainly the most exotic. One-to-three bedroom suites, all with marble bathrooms, full kitchens, three swimming pools, and ocean-view rooms. The advantage of this Mexican hotel chain is a suite for the price of a Marriott or Sheraton hotel room. This brand new 5-star resort advertises a 4 day/3 night package for less than $400.00, as of this writing. Call 800-659-8477 or directly to the hotel at 322-10091 or fax 322-10755. Note: to call direct to Puerto Vallarta, Mexico from the U.S., you need to dial 011-52-322-xxxxx.

Main Beach Area

A few miles south of the airport, this is the major hotel development area with a great beach and all the amenities of a grand resort.

Playa de Oro Beach Adjacent to the Marina, this is a mid-class hotel, the first on hotel row, with some nifty time-share pent-houses. A good choice if you're on a budget. The tour agent of your airline can book it for you. (In Mexico, call 52-322-20348)

Krystal Designed like a Mexican village of individual suites and bungalows set in a Roman courtyard complete with a huge Olympic-style pool that overflows into the ocean. Inside this enormous pool are man-made sun-chairs so you can lie in the water, get tan, order drinks, and never move. This is the best property of Mexico's second-best hotel chain: a 37-acre oasis with 44 individual swimming pools for the private bungalow units. It even has its own bull-ring for the fiesta. In addition to the tropical gardens, the best disco in town, **Christina's**, is adjacent to this property. By the way, Krystal frequently offers a promotional: book three nights, get a fourth night free. This is my choice. (800-231-9860)

Fiesta Americana The best hotel chain in Mexico with at least four properties in Puerto Vallarta. The first, called Fiesta America, features a gigantic palapa-domed (straw) lobby and is on the best part of Los Tules beach. Next is the Condesa Spa, brand new with complete European spa facilities, but right in the middle of hotel row. Last on the list and probably the most fun but full of noise hotel in the chain is the Plaza Vallarta, which offers a John Newcombe tennis center with indoor courts and planned activities for all ages. The water aerobics is an easy way to make new friends: just pick out the perfect spot (be sure to wait for the class to begin and then join in) and act helpless! Staying at any of these hotels would be my choice, since not only can you use all of their facilities, but pool-hopping makes meeting new friends that much easier.

If you own a time-share, this is the place to do your exchange, since their Los Tules condos, situated between the hotels, are the class act in Puerto Vallarta. (800-223-2332 or 800-FIESTA-1)

Sheraton Bouganvilias The farthest south of the hotels, it is within walking distance of the town. At one time this was the grandest hotel in town, and in many ways it still is with the new time-share condominiums recently finished. With over 500 rooms housed on six floors, and flowers hanging over the balconies, it also offers a new time-share condo arrangement, making this a solid choice. (800-325-3535)

Omni Next door to the Fiesta Americana Hotel, this is certainly the most opulent, new hotel in this beach area. There's a tennis court on the second floor and a grand spa, including full aerobics, weights, life-cycles, stairmasters, and you name it. Suites are available for the discriminating traveler. (800-THE-OMNI)

Chapter 4

Playa Conchas Chinas Beach Area

This beach area south of Puerto Vallarta proper has many small bungalows, cheaper hotels, and home and condominium rentals. Half an hour from the airport, but full of charm with a good beach. One recommended hotel is:

Tres Vidas Three villas climbing up a hillside with a total of 5,000 square feet each. The living rooms open onto the ocean. These three-bedroom villas include a cook who prepares breakfast and dinner and does your shopping. There is also a roof-top swimming pool and a beautiful view of the bay. Locally owned. Rates as low as $130 in low season. (714-723-6353)

A Tip on Booking Your Hotel Before you go, I suggest that you check out the Sunday Travel section of the major newspapers to find the best packages. In addition to the deals offered by your travel agent, the airlines have some tremendous promotionals and tie-ins with the major hotels. If you pre-pay for a package tour, try for the minimum stay, normally three days. If you can spend more time, shop around for a good deal. You may find that you are unhappy with your location or that you just want to try someplace different. Due to all the new construction, you can always find a room. The best of the tour operators are:

> **Reforma Mexico** 800-242-4436
>
> **Mexico Tourism Consultants** 800-252-0100
>
> **Empire Tours** 800-833-3333

TRAVELING AROUND

Taxis are your major form of transportation. All have set prices and there is no haggling, but it never hurts to try. They are usually easy to find, but late at night the price doubles. From the main beach hotel row to downtown is 10,000 pesos ($3.50), and from the Marina area to downtown is 16,000 pesos ($6).

WHAT TO DO

This is truly the place to beach it. Life centers on the beach, if not for flirting, sunning, playing sports, then for going shopping. Your best bargains are found among the beach vendors, but be careful about the quality and do bargain with them. A good trick is to watch the person before you purchase what you want and then you have a good idea of a bottom price. Wait for a crowd and be a patient observer.

As for the best beach, it really depends on your mood. First, try in front of your hotel for convenience; then try the beach by the Fiesta America and the Holiday Inn where you get the widest expanse of sand with comfy surroundings. If you want to try something different, take a cab to **Playa Los Muertos** (Dead Man's Beach) south of town, where it's more bohemian, with many locals, students, and secretaries from Guadalajara. This is definitely the beach to party on, have lunch, and get away from the American and Canadian tourists. You can always return to your beach on hotel row if you don't feel comfortable here.

Another favorite activity is traveling to the islands. **Yelpa**, my favorite, can be reached on the cruise ship Sarape (550 passengers) or the Princess Yelpa (300 passen-

Main Beach Area

gers), departing daily at around 9:00 A.M. from the Marina Pier. On this island you can swim, ride horseback, hike to an isolated town where many people have never been to the mainland, have a fresh fish fry on the beach, or just take in the tropical surroundings. As you depart from the boat, a small child will become your guide and lead you to your choice activity and perhaps sell you a picture with an iguana. The best part of this trip are the pies made on the island; the lemon, coconut, and pecan nut cakes are the best I've ever had—perhaps as good as sex.

Seven miles south of Puerto Vallarta is **Mismaloya Beach**, where "Night of the Iguana" was filmed. Here you can rent canoes, hike, or search for huge turtles. About two miles off the highway is **Chino's Paradise**, built around huge boulders, where you can swim in natural pools and have a lunch of lobster, shrimp, octopus, and filet for less than twenty dollars. If you don't have a car (easily rentable in town), there are always taxis to take you back and forth.

You can also rent scooters to get a feel for the area. This is a perfect way to check out the new marina hotels, the Marriott and Melia. For those of you who like to shop for clothes, try the Aca Joe store on the **Malecon** (the board-walk). Speaking of the Malecon, be there for the evening sunsets. Every night is different, and there is always a group watching the day's end. Sunset watching may not be as popular as it is in Key West, where it's the main event, but it's certainly as beautiful. The Malecon, which runs along the coast, is perfect for that evening sea walk where much flirting, bar-hopping, and people watching take place. It's only a short stroll over the river to **Gringo Gulch**, where most of the retired Americans live and Elizabeth Taylor and Richard Burton once called home.

A note on one last activity, **pool-hopping**: this is an important element in your trip, for if your pool is full of loud and drunk party types or is inhabited by couples, it's time to look for a new place to hang out. My expertise in this art comes from my obsession of finding square pools in which to swim laps. The trick is always to look and act as though you "belong." Order lunch or a drink if you find an interest-ing-looking pool (if not square, perhaps full of vacationing airline stewardesses) and make yourself at home. I've never been asked to leave, for all hotels love to have people eating and drinking around the pool. This is a great money-maker for them; they feel if one person orders, others will follow. Remember, if you're staying at one of the Fiesta Americanas, you can charge and play at them all.

WOMEN AND NIGHTLIFE

There are three main choices for meeting women: discos, bars, and hotel entertainment.

Discos

It seems that the late night disco is still very big in Mexico, and they have their share of exotic and outrageous dance floors. The main in-town discos are **City Dump**, which is the oldest and most popular; **Sundance**, the biggest; and **Capriccio's**, the jet-set hang-out, catering to the better dressed chic crowd. For a laid-back, wear-anything type of disco, **The Zoo** is the place to go. The newest is **Christine's**, where the light show, lasers, strobes, and architecture make this place a must-see even if you hate the music. Its location next to the Krystal Hotel allows you to escape the deafening music to one of the quieter hotel bars for a breather. For transportation to and from town, use a taxi. The good news is that you won't have a problem finding one; the bad news is that after some unknown hour the rates double.

Bars

As for bars, there is only one name to remember, **Carlos O'Briens**. On the Malecon, this is the action spot of Puerto Vallarta, and the chain is the same all over Mexico. Usually there are long lines to get into the bar during prime evening hours, so tell the "bouncer" you're there for dinner. Go upstairs, order a salad (the food isn't the best, but you're not here for the food) and a beer, peer over the balcony, and choose a prime location next to some of those vacationing schoolteachers. Once downstairs, you can't hear, see, smell anything and away you go! This place is famous for ladies dancing on the tables, shooting tequila shots with the waiters encouraging everything imaginable. If you can think of it, it will happen at Carlos O'Brien's sooner or later.

Next door is the more mellow **Casablanca**, if Carlos's is too much for you. Just down the street past Aca Joe clothing store is the newest hot-spot in town, the **Hard Rock Cafe**. Besides good food and good air-conditioning (you can get very hot walking the boardwalk in 98% humidity), a band starts at 10.00 P.M. and the craziness begins. This new cafe has become so popular that the lines at Carlos O'Briens have started to disappear. My favorite place to hang out is **Friday Lopez's**, where the music is easy to

dance to, the atmosphere casual, and the company a little more mature. Also its location at the Fiesta Americana Hotel makes it the perfect late-night stop.

There is no red-light district that is easily accessible. The taxi drivers know of places, if you're interested, but they're usually an hour ride to who knows where. You have to go to the next town, called **Juan**, in the adjacent state. This is a raunchy place, best left for the cowboys. If you must go, make sure some locals are with you who understand the language and customs. I think the best plan is to find a nice working girl (the one at your front desk who changes the money or the one who rents a "free Jeep" if you come to the time-share presentations) and ask her out for dinner and dancing. For her, this is a special treat, as in a resort town like Puerto Vallarta this is a very expensive night out.

As for those time-share salesmen who promise you anything (or anyone) they have a wealth of information on the seedy side of Puerto Vallarta. Besides explaining why you'll come back year after year, they want to make sure you have a good time. I love the free breakfasts and free one-day jeeps, and then after the presentation I say I'm a lawyer in the States and they run for cover! Another way out is to say you're a real-estate salesman and then they know you have all the answers. Remember, these people are just trying to make a living, so treat them with respect and caution, as they usually carry loads of good information regarding the new "in" bars, the discos, the cheap rent-a-cars and hotels, and the best tennis spots. They may even be able to tell you where those airline stewardesses are staying.

If a sports-bar is your taste, you won't be disappointed in Puerto Vallarta. **The Alamo**, at the south end of the Malecon in the cul-de-sac, has three satellite televisions and the 45-incher is always tuned to the latest sports happening. Besides good drinks, the food upstairs is fantastic with perfect views of the ocean and the commotion on the Malecon.

A tip about making new female friends: when you see the big cruise ships sailing into the Marina, the passengers will disembark and go directly to the Krystal Hotel's enormous pool and beach. Just walk in, order lunch, and pretend you're a cruise passenger, and with some luck you'll be surrounded by a few hundred lonely females.

A LUSTY ADVENTURE: THE ROAD TO MANZANILLO

One of my more interesting side trips in Mexico included a drive between Puerto Vallarta and Manzanillo. Most people fly the 150 miles, but the drive — four hours without stops — is full of natural beauty, lush resorts, forgotten beaches and a taste a real Mexico. Although there is an international airport 25 miles north of Manzanillo, flying doesn't beat the drive and the reward —a unique city, untouched by tourists, most of whom are on the beaches 10 miles north of town.

Chapter 4

Little has changed in this seaport since the early 1600's when it was the Spanish gateway to the Philippines. Here you'll find a historic "red-light zone" with funky bars, dressed-to-sell prostitutes, and colorful characters. Manzanillo is Mexico's most important port — it relies on loaded ships and content *men* for its economical survival.

Leaving Puerto Vallarta from the south, you can head towards Manzanillo on Highway 200. There is only one road and for the first 80 miles you travel further from the ocean, reaching altitudes close to 3,000 feet. You'll encounter lush tropical scenery, runaway cattle and horses, kids with their chickens, and small rest-stops. Here, the curious villagers offer drinks and local food. At Chamela, less than 100 miles from Puerto Vallarta, the route descends back to the ocean and runs along the coast. Interesting stops include: **Hotel Plaza Careyes**, a few miles past Chamela, a perfect spot for lunch and a swim. Set in the crystal clear waters of Careyes Bay, the hotel is subdued and luxurious; also **Hotel Fiesta Americana at Los Angeles Loccos de Tenacatita**, situated on a deserted golden beach, a few miles from the highway and traversed by a cobblestone road, the 240 room self-contained contemporary hotel and entertainment complex is 35 miles north of the Manzanillo Airport; **Barra de Navidad,** a laid back town with dirt roads that remind one of a beach village in the wild west. It was here in 1564 that an expedition of Spanish galleons left to conquer the Philippine Islands. Nothing much has changed except the beauty of its crescent-shaped beach, which has become a tourist attraction. The fish restaurants are some of the best in Mexico.

Although the highway appears deserted, be careful not to drive too fast, as hidden in the bushes are the notorious Mexican Highway Patrol on the lookout for speeders, stolen cars, and drug carriers. Always (and I mean always) carry your registration in your glove box! When the MHP stopped me, I had misplaced the rental car registration. My broken Spanish made my explanation difficult. When renting a car in Mexico, ask for a day and night telephone number of the rental company, carry the agent's card, and make sure there is a *current* registration with the rental car company's name on it.

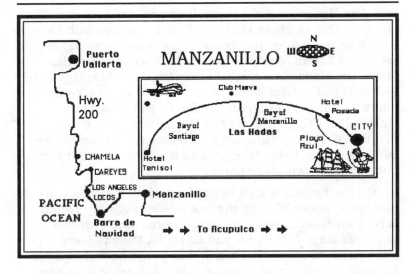

To shorten the drive, try an open-jaws ticket (done easily with a Mexican carrier) and a one way car rental. For example, you might land in Puerto Vallarta, drive to Manzanillo, and then fly back to the U.S. from Manzanillo airport. The trick is to find a cheap but reliable one-way car rental — preferably one of the national chains with counters at the airport. (AHMSA and Odin are Mexican chains that have the lowest prices, but make sure to check their cars or jeeps carefully!) Pemex gas stations are common in the populated areas (every 30 to 40 miles) but never run below a quarter tank of gas: sometimes the stations are closed for the day.

As you approach the Bay of Manzanillo from the north (first comes the airport - a good 25 miles from city center), you'll pass two smaller bays with spectacular beaches: **Bahia de Santiago**, famous for the Las Hadas complex and **Bahia de Manzanillo**, known as the bay where the cargo ships enter opposite Playa Azul beach. My favorite place to stay is the **Tenisol Hotel**, situated on the first beach of Bahia de Santiago because of its three uninterrupted miles of flat beach for my runs. The hotel has time-share suites that rent for half the price of a Las Hadas hotel room. There is a great golf and tennis club where you can meet Mexican businessmen rather than tourists from Canada (800-525-1987)! Of course, you can stay at the deluxe *Westin* property, **Las Hadas,** at $200 to $300 a night, (local phone 333-300-00). This is where Dudley Moore fell in love with Bo Derick in the movie "10." Some of the neighboring hotels are **Hotel Sierra Manzanillo** and the **Plaza Las Glorias**. Above Las Hadas is a huge 90-acre Greek-style village hotel, with 500 units, time-share opportunities, and a nice entertainment complex promoted as the largest resort in Manzanillo, called **Club Maeva** (local phone 305-95 or 800-223-0888). Not only are there 12 tennis courts, one of the largest pools in Latin America and the best disco in town, but it has its own water park!

On the far end of this Bay is Playa Azul which is connected to "Route 200" by the Las Brisas Highway. Found here is an endless string of budget hotels, the best two being the **Days Inn Motel** and **Hotel La Posada** (local phone 333-224-04). This beach area is the perfect location for that one wild night in town. It is a few miles from city center, with an endless beach as its porch and a lagoon for the backyard.

The town of Manzanillo is not distinctive. Tourists come to this area for the fabulous beaches and tropical scenery. But for the adventurous male, the city provides a bonus: besides few tourists, inexpensive seafood restaurants (half the price that of Puerto Vallarta), and a picturesque Plaza Principal, there is a an old time seafaring "red light district," just like the movies. I will never forget that night in Manzanillo! I had heard rumors of such a place. In order to find this **"lusty fun zone,"** I used a technique I learned in Uruguay. Once, hopelessly lost in my rental car, on the backroads of Montevideo I asked a taxi cab for directions, to which he replied "follow me." I did and finally found the beach. When you are lost in a foreign country simply ask to follow a cab - pay half before and half upon arriving! We soon spotted the ladies in mini-skirts and loud music. It was at the far southeast end of town, a few miles from the seafront.

The atmosphere in the bars was unbelievable, reminiscent of an eigth grade sock-hop. The men were on one side of the sawdust floor and the ladies (all dressed to kill or capture alive) were huddled in the other corner. Only a brave "hombre" would dare to ask a lady to dance and ask her "price." Once he returned to the male gallery, he would be interrogated about the dangerous crossing. It wasn't the place to show our manliness, so my friend and I decided to leave and check the street action. Not drawing much attention, we decided these girls weren't for us and decided to leave. As we approached our car, the prettiest street walker came up and propositioned my friend and made an offer he couldn't refuse — $20 and a private room. Since I was left out, she immediately offered a friend ... same deal, same room but an unseen girl. Not to be a party pooper I said "sure, who knows if this could be my lucky night!"

I was designated to go first after the coin flip. I was introduced to my partner - a short, freckled twenty-two year old in a mini-skirt. The room was the size of an airline bathroom with a table covered with 50 shades of make-up, and a mirror strung with hanging fishnet stockings. The closet was stuffed with red and black mini-skirts, and alas, a small fan to cool the 90-degree room. As she took her clothes off, I realized I had made a big mistake .... she must have had four kids (the two girdles hid the blubber well) and her body was coverd with tattoos! Nothing is more embarrassing for a man than to not react to a naked girl standing in front of him! I apologized, said it was the spoiled fish I had for dinner, paid my $20, and left. Meanwhile, my friend waited impatiently outside. It was his turn and he had an exhilarating time, unaware of my embarrassing experience.

I'll never forget that humid night, as I realized that it is often the window shopping, browsing, and flirting which are exciting, not the sex! To this day, that night governs my travel plans: the fun is the people, not the sex. Foreign destinations must have something more than virtueless girls, a girl must have something more to offer than just being naked!! The next time you are in Manzanillo, try Carlos'n Charlie's at the Las Hadas Junction, but beware of freckled-face girls in tight, tight mini skirts!

Chapter 4

GETTING HOME

Allow plenty of time to check out, for the cashier seems to take an hour to add up your bill, then invariably forgets something or decides he doesn't have enough money to make change for you. Also, reconfirm at least a few days before returning; the computers in Mexico run a little slower, and you could easily just disappear. If the phones are busy, the airlines, banks, and consulates are in the center of town — a few minutes by cab.

The ride to the airport takes only a few minutes by taxi, but arrive early, for if something may go wrong, it will in Mexico. Believe it or not, once I was meeting my sister in Puerto Vallarta; she was coming from San Francisco and I from Los Angeles. While we were in the air, they decided to work on the runway in Puerto Vallarta and diverted us to Mazatlan. My sister and I were allowed to wave at each other but not talk, for though we were waiting for hours at the same airport, we weren't allowed to go through customs since we were not legally in Mexico yet. When we did land in Puerto Vallarta, the customs had to handle eight planes simultaneously, all of which had been waiting some place in Mexico to finally land. This was not the beginnings of a good trip, though the rest of it was fine.

Part 2
A Little Farther
and More Fun

- Costa Rica

- Dominican Republic

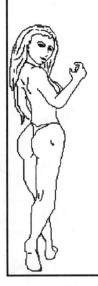

Costa Rica

I had wanted to travel to Costa Rica ever since I was in high school, but until a short while ago, the destination eluded me. I had heard it was like a little Switzerland of Central America with no army, a lush landscape, pristine beaches, friendly people, and of course those beautiful "Tico" women. The problem was that Costa Rica was not close to any other place I wanted to visit, and so I never got there even though when I travel I try to see as much as I can and stop at interesting places on my way to my main destination. But one morning I woke up to a full page ad in the Los Angeles Times offering "triple" miles to South America, and a new low airfare, so off I went.

An increasing number of travelers are likewise discovering Costa Rica, not only as a tourist destination but as a place to live. As a result there are cut-rate fares and many tour operators who specialize in packaged trips to Costa Rica. Not only does this country have a temperate climate due to its location between two oceans but most of the people live within 75 miles of the coastline. An added bonus to this special place is that the national parks, which take up more than 12% of the country's territory, are complete with rain forests, marshes, coral reefs, volcanoes, caves, geothermal springs and man-grove swamps. Even the prices at hotels and restaurants are moderate and the tap water is safe to drink.

But what is truly special is the people. Ticos, as Costa Ricans are called, are educated, yet simple, likeable people. Instead of pouring funds into an elaborate defense system, the government has spent most of its money on education and medical services. Being helpful is their way of life. Costa Rica is one of the few democracies in Central America, and the people pride themselves as being a special

Chapter 5

breed with a strong national identity. Here the combination of a Caribbean coast, tropical jungles, hidden valleys and waterfalls, and an untapped Pacific Coast that one day will rival Mexico's Riviera make the country a marvelous adventure. No wonder more than 20,000 Americans have retired here.

A little known fact is the origin of the country's name. It is said that Christopher Columbus, on his fourth voyage to the New World in 1502, was blown into a small shelter on the Caribbean coast. Here, in the port city of Limon, he encountered Indians wearing jewelry and gold and was convinced he found a land of untold wealth. He named the coast, Costa Rica (rich coast).

GETTING THERE

United Airlines has direct flights to Costa Rica from the West coast. United flight #889 leaves Los Angeles at 11.20 P.M., makes a short stop in Guatemala City, and then arrives in San Jose, Costa Rica at 8.40 A.M. the following morning. American Airlines bought out the old Eastern Airlines routes and is my second choice. The last U.S. carrier is Continental.

There are also three Central/South American airlines that offer cheaper fares: LACSA (800-225-2272); Mexicana (800-531-7923); and the Costa Rican carrier TACA (800-535-8780). These airlines have connections from Los Angeles, Houston, New Orleans, and New York. You may sometimes see unbelievably low fares, but there is usually a catch. For example, recently some tour operators were promoting a $299 round-trip flight from Los Angeles, but the plane left at midnight, you had to buy their hotel package, and the plane spent an eight-hour lay-over in Guatemala City (although they were offering a free tour of the city).

Using an Agency

If you prefer to use an agency, here are three good ones that specialize in flights to Costa Rica and hotel bookings:

Tourtech Their speciality is a one-week tour, currently for $565 from Los Angeles. They also offer combination trips which include Manuel Antonio Beach Park, car rentals, as well as special Christmas and New Year's trips. The beach-and-city combos have good prices. (800-882-2636).

H.I.S. International Tours They offer low-cost flights, $299 from Los Angeles. (213-613-0943).

EcoTours 3325 Wilshire Blvd., Suite 504, Los Angeles 90010. (800-882-1885).

Tracks to Costa Rica 42-446 Bob Hope Drive, Suite 105, Rancho Mirage 92270. (800-273-5759).

CLIMATE

The dry season for western Costa Rica, where you'll spend most of your time, is December through April, and corresponds to their summer. San Jose is situated in a valley and is usually mild, but in the evenings you may need a sweater. The west coast is much like Acapulco: hot

and humid. If you visit a little before or after the dry season, expect rain and more rain from June to November. In June it rains four to five times as much as it does in May.

ABOUT THE CITY OF SAN JOSE

The city of San Jose will be the center of your trip. Situated in a valley surrounded by beautiful mountains, this modern, high rise city is overpopulated because of the many illegal aliens from bordering countries who gather here looking for work. The city, however, is a charming metropolitan center. A combination of modern and Spanish architecture makes this a fascinating place to walk. At night everyone strolls around the parks, gossips with friends, snacks, and has a good time. This is a wonderful night city.

San Jose is the largest city in Costa Rica and is laid out in angular ways and streets with crisscrossing avenues. Almost exactly in the center of the country, this city is the perfect spot to call homebase, from which you can decide which beach or tour to take. Travel agents, car rental firms, hotels and tour operators are everywhere. Three other cities are also in the central valley: Heredia, Alajuela,and Cartago. The most important coastal cities include Puntarenas to the west, Limon to the east and Nicoya to the north.

WHERE TO STAY

After going through customs at the airport, you might as well simply take a taxi to your hotel. As you go upstairs into the arrival hall, expect to be mauled by kids offering to take you to a taxi. Don't fight it: take your pick. The following are my recommendations for hotels:

Holiday Inn Ultra-modern with a 17-story glass landmark and all the amenities. The only five-star property in San Jose, this is the most logical choice of hotels if you must be in the center of things. The hotel faces Morazan Park and is near all major government and commercial offices as well as shopping and entertainment areas. (800-HOLIDAY)

Sheraton Called the Herradura, this is a country club hotel with condos, a golf course, but practically no feeling of being in Costa Rica. Remember, we are here to meet the people, but if you want to jet-set, this is the place. (800-325-3535)

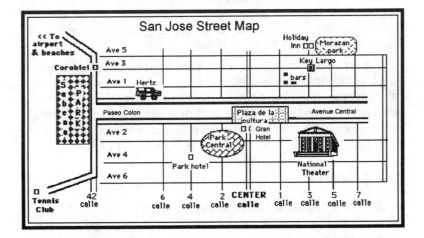

San Jose Street Map

Gran Hotel This hotel's inner courts and gardens overlooking Plaza de la Cultura is the perfect people-watching area, in front of the National Theater. Has a small casino and adequate rooms, but the location makes this a top choice. (21-4000; first dial the access number for Costa Rica from the U.S. 011-506; they can fax back immediate *written* confirmation like most hotels).

Garden Court Highly recommended budget hotel. Carpets, television, telephone, 70 air-conditioned rooms, huge American breakfast. Currently $29 for a single, $35 for a double. Write Apartado 962-1000, San Jose, Costa Rica.

Tennis Club Away from the hustle of downtown (just a 30-minute stroll down Paseo Colon, the main east-west street), the Tennis Club is my first choice for San Jose. You get a full tennis club with professionals and ballboys, two Olympic pools, a basketball court, and a huge park across the street with a lake and running paths. Have you ever wondered what is done with those old, useless airports? This park (Sabena Park) is the old San Jose airport before jets arrived. What a marvelous idea and fantastic execution. (Why can't we do this in our country? It seems that wherever one travels outside the States, there are such great parks for people to walk, flirt, and fall in love.) But speaking of the Tennis Club, why not reserve a mini-suite facing the mountains? It's only a few dollars more. (32-1266 or fax 506-32-3867). The front desk is very helpful and can tell you where you can find anything.

Aparthotel Ramgo If a big pool is not important and you like the idea of no one watching whom you bring in or take out (or how many times), this is the place for you. You get a small apartment, quiet and discreet, for the price of a room. Located a block west of the Tennis Club and across from Sabena Park. (32-3366 or fax 506-32-3111)

CAR RENTALS

Hertz is probably the best place to rent a car. However, it seems much cheaper to reserve your car after you arrive than to use the toll-free U. S. reservation numbers. Remember, these agencies are independently owned, so one Hertz (or Avis or Budget, etc.) rate will differ from another. On your walk downtown there will be half-a-dozen car rental agencies, so start checking. I found Hertz on Paseo Colon (23-5959) one hundred dollars cheaper than the others. Sooner or later you'll need a car to visit the beaches and to do some extensive sight-seeing.

ODDS AND ENDS

Although a visit to Costa Rica sounds exotic, in reality it's similar to being in Mexico, only cleaner. There are a few basic things one should know about Costa Rica. First, many people speak English here, so if you don't speak Spanish, no problema! Next, your hotel and food bill will include a 20% service charge: 10% sales tax and 10% service. If the service is extra good, you may add an extra 10%. Also, the electric current is the same as ours. Costa Rica is on Central time, but does not have daylight-savings time. You'll be able to read U.S.A. Today as well as watch CNN in the better hotels, and once a week a Tico Times is published in English, explaining the local news as well as containing advertisements for restaurants, night clubs, and cultural activities. One last word of advice: don't be lulled into the idea that this little Switzerland has no crime. This is absolutely wrong. Apparently many Nicaraguans fleeing their country's woes enter Costa Rica illegally and have no means of support. The good news is that they don't mug or maim; the bad news that they may steal everything from your car, including the spare tire and jack. Be cautious and don't take unnecessary chances.

Stop for a beer at a local tavern and you will be presented with a "boca". These tidbits are free food and may be fried beef, chicken, or barbecued pork in a tortilla. Boca means "mouth" and you can actually make a complete meal from these inexpensive treats. At roadside stands in San Jose and on the coast you can buy fresh coconuts and pipas, which are green coconuts sold with a straw to drink the sweet juice. The chayote is a squash that when steamed and buttered are the regional side dish as popular as our french fries.

WHAT TO DO IN SAN JOSE

What I find special about being in San Jose is the people, and the feeling of being in a happy environment. San Jose is a walking city. Be sure to see the elegant **National Theater**, patterned after a European opera house in the Renaissance style, on Avenida 2, Calles 3 and 5; and the **National Museum** in the old Bellavista Fortress; the Plaza de la Cultura with its pre-Columbian artifacts underground. By the way, the tourist office is also at the Plaza de la Cultura, where you can get maps, trip ideas, and general information.

A word on directions: avenues (**avenidas**) run east-west; streets (**calles**) run north-south. Even-numbered avenidas are to the south of Paseo Colon; even-numbered calles are to the west of the main streets. Sounds simple? It's not, for

Chapter 5

many streets aren't marked. So do as I did: if you are looking for a special place, count. By the way, Paseo Colon
turns into Avenida Central as you walk from Sabena Park.

As for shopping, the best buys are handcrafted items
such as plates, bowls, and chairs made from unusual
woods like cedar, cocobolo, and laurel. On the center
streets (Paseo Colon and Avenida Central) you will find
many reproductions of pre-Columbian gold and silver
pieces. More fun are the street vendors with whom you can
bargain.

One added bonus for some travelers is that Costa Rica
has legalized gambling in selected hotels and casinos, but
the games are the same as we play here, and with a little
luck you can make this a profitable trip.

TOUR TRIPS OUT OF SAN JOSE

The main tourist attractions are the parks, natural
wildlife preserves, and beaches. For organized tours from
San Jose, you can get half-day tours for $50 or less; full-
day tours for less than $100. Try bargaining if you're visit-
ing in the off-season. The best tours are as follows:

Irazu Volcano The most popular, half-day tour in Costa
Rica. You leave San Jose, heading southeast. First you see
the old capital city of Cartago, then climb the black slopes
of the volcano, passing through the most important potato-
producing area of the country. You climb to the top, 11,324
feet, where on a clear day you can see both the Pacific and
the Atlantic.

Pacific Island Cruise This is a full-day trip. The bus
leaves early in the morning for Puntarenas where you board
a cruise boat (usually the 50-foot Calypso, safe and relaxing) that takes you toward the islands in the Gulf of Nicoya.
You stop at a beautiful, white sand beach, where after
lunch you can snorkel or sun bathe.

White Water Rafting A full-day tour that starts at 6:45
A.M. First the bus takes you through the beautiful Orosi
Valley to Tucurrique. Here you start 12 miles of shooting
the rapids, with short periods of calm water to catch your
breath. The trip takes nine hours and once back to your
hotel you are totally exhausted.

Jungle Train Tour A full-day tour by narrow-gauge railway through the jungle to the eastern side of the country. This track, completed in 1891, takes you through the cool central plateau to the steamy rain forest near the coast. You follow the Reventazon River and watch the people work on the banana, cocoa, and coconut plantations. A bus takes you back to San Jose. Lunch is included. A one-day extension to Limon can be arranged that includes a night in a hotel.

AMAZING PARKS, GARDENS, AND FORESTS

In addition to the above organized tours, be sure to take some time to visit some of Costa Rica's natural wonders. Known as the garden spot of the Americas, Costa Rica's national park system, with 28 national parks and 10 recreational, extends over 12% of the country.

In **Tortuguero Park** on the Caribbean coast, huge sea turtles lay their eggs from August to October. **Cocos Island National Park** is the largest uninhabited island in the world, at 20 square miles, with hundreds of waterfalls and coral reefs rich with marine life including sharks, dolphins, and tuna. Only on Cocos Island will you see the Cocos finch, Ridgeway flycatcher, and the cuckoo.

Speaking of birds, Costa Rica has 848 species, more than can be found in all of North America north of Mexico. Heavy rainfall (over 200 inches in some mountain areas) and a wide variety of elevation zones (sea level to 12,530 feet) account for the abundance of bird species. If natural beauty is important to you, you can't go wrong in Costa Rica.

THE BEACHES: WHERE TO GO AND STAY

There are tour packages to get you to and from beaches if you are staying in San Jose, but I truly recommend that you rent a car and drive yourself. Up north in the Guanacaste area are some of the country's most beautiful beaches. As you make your way along the Pan American Highway, you'll see large cattle ranches and endless hills, making you think you're in Arizona. Towns like Liberia and Nicoya make interesting stops on the way to the northern beaches.

Flamingo Beach is the new in-spot for beach lovers, and airplane flights are available if the long drive doesn't interest you. Located in the northwest section of the country.

Playa Hermosa is another area you might want to investigate, where for the elite the **Condovac La Costa** offers 101 villas climbing up a green mountain with exceptional views of the Gulf of Papagayo. You can book in San Jose at 21-8949. A second choice in the Playa Hermosa area is the **Coca Beach Guanacaste Hotel** (67-0283), not as elegant but just as enjoyable.

The Southern Beaches: Puntarenas, Jaco Beach (Playa Jaco), and Surroundings:

This area is my choice for a one-week vacation: three days in San Jose and four days driving to the southern beaches and surrounding area. Not only is the drive easy and colorful, but on your return you pass the airport, where you can return your rent-a-car and never have to re-enter San Jose, unless you need to say goodbye to a loved one. Following the Pan American Route 1 out of San Jose, you travel through tropical vegetation down to the port city of Puntarenas, where you can either stay a day or so or continue on to Jaco Beach.

Puntarenas juts out into the Gulf of Nicoya, and since there is only one road to the end, it's hard to get lost. Many beach bars line the road, and at night it's quite fun. The beach isn't the best, but two great hotels make the stop pleasant.

Hotel Porto Bello A tropical paradise with two swimming pools, international cuisine, yacht tours to the bay, and facilities for sport fishing. (61-1322 or fax 506-61-0036).

Fiesta Hotel and Casino If Puntarenas seems a little seedy and dirty for you, then try this brand new, 140-room hotel outside of town with its own clean beach. It offers cablevision, a full gym, bikes, and facilities for sailing, fishing, sea kayaking, wind-surfing, and scuba-diving. (39-4266 or fax 506-39-0217). They will provide transportation from San Jose if you don't want to drive. One day or night in Puntarenas is enough. There is only one road out of town: straight ahead is back to San Jose; to the left, the Guanacaste area (towards Liberia); and to the right, Jaco Beach.

Manuel Antonio Park is also in the southern part of the province. This beautiful national park and its awesome beach are about an hour and a half (depending on the road construction) beyond Jaco Beach. You can find a wide variety of accommodations here. **Quepos**, the main city, is 95 miles east of San Jose. My recommendation is that you use Jaco as your base for exploring the region, as here are the best hotels, restaurants, and things to do for the single male. To reach Jaco, you can follow the Costanera (the new road from Puntarenas south) or you can choose the slower, scenic road with breathtaking hilltop views through Atenas, Mateo, and Orotina. The best solution is a circle tour, so you see more country and avoid repetition.

A word of caution: *even though cars pass you left and right, drive patiently and carefully. Getting stuck behind the trucks and buses on these two-lane, hilly, curvy roads is frustrating, but it's better to arrive late than mangled.*

Chapter 5

Jaco Beach is the most developed beach area in Costa Rica. This doesn't mean it has the best beach; in fact, the beach is of gray volcanic sand and looks menacing. When the tide goes out, the scenery changes to a mystical lava look, perfect for those long runs or walks. The town (more of a village) is about three miles long and full of quaint little restaurants, my favorite being the **Star of David** with its excellent seafood and low prices, across from the Fiesta Jaco. Countless boutiques, discos, bars, and lobby bars make this the best area for the single male. The bad news is that most people here are Canadians or Germans, so in order to find the charming Tico women you may need to go back to San Jose.

Here's a list of places to stay in the area:

Jaco Beach Hotel If you don't like the idea of driving, the Jaco Beach Hotel has complementary bus service from San Jose when you book the room. This is a commercial hotel, full of tourists, but it's located right on the beach, has full facilities, and a large cable T.V. in the lobby, where I watched the Gulf War updates on CNN. In San Jose call 32-4811 or Telex 2307 IRAZU CR.

El Jardin Hotel sits smack in the middle of town and is, as its name suggests, a beautiful garden. 64-3050.

Fiesta Jaco, brand new, to the south of the village and away from the motorcycle exhaust, is my choice of hotels here. It's full of Canadians (since it was built by a Canadian developer), but its location and sports facilities can't be beat. The rooms are extra large with separate laundry facilities in the mini-suites. The sunsets are spectacular here and the European chef is a tennis player. Follow the signs, as it's a little outside of town and a quick right.

Beyond Jaco Beach is the beach in **Manuel Antonio Park**, considered the best beach in all of Costa Rica because you have to make your way through a jungle full of animals, swamps, exotic plants (and rugged Canadian and German hikers). There are three beaches that get better, and more isolated, the farther you go until you reach a pristine bay, perfect for snorkeling or reading a book that you haven't started yet. While I was there an earthquake occurred, but being from southern California I considered it just another day in paradise. This trip, an hour and a half from Jaco Beach, provides an opportunity to experience a rare harmony among the jungle, the animals, and the ocean.

On your way to Manuel Antonio Park, you can pick from these hotels:

Hotel La Mariposa, situated high on a bluff overlooking the Pacific between Quepos and Manuel Antonio Park, this is the most exotic hotel in Costa Rica. This hotel offers adults-only villas with balconies, indoor gardens, flowers everywhere, and a pool with a view of the valley. This is truly the perfect spot if you have met Miss Right in San Jose. (77-0355 or fax 506-77-0050).

Hotel Karahe, which adjoins the national park and has a unique pool separate from the hotel directly on the beach, is another good choice. Each bungalow has its own refrigerator and a good view of the beach, which is only a short walk away. (77-0170 or fax 506-77-0152).

WOMEN AND NIGHTLIFE

I remember a few years ago reading a Costa Rica travel book warning American men about Tico women. So if you think you're ready to retire to a less hectic, cheaper life-style in Costa Rica, let me explain what I learned. If you like Costa Rica, sooner or later you will meet a

Chapter 5

beautiful, spell-binding Tico woman. During the courtship, she will do anything to make you feel special. You may start to think about getting married, having a family, but you aren't prepared for the Costa Rican family way of life. Children, schooling, and in-laws will gradually become more important to your Tico wife than anything, even more important than you. And if your love should end and the divorce proceedings begin, oh do the Costa Rican lawyers have a field day with their Gringo prize. Now, with that warning, let us proceed.

In our foreign travels we will run across three basic types of women: 1. good girls; 2. bad girls; 3. good girls, who with a little persuasion become bad girls. Let me explain.

I remember walking the boardwalk in Rio when a young girl in a mini-skirt, sitting on the bench, opened her legs (she wasn't wearing underwear) and asked, "do you want it?" Obviously a "bad girl." On the other hand, I also re-member a secretary I met on a beach in the Dominican Republic, who for a nice dinner and a night of dancing and staying in a plush resort made me her Prince Charming. This was more so a case of a good girl being persuaded to become a bad girl. In Costa Rica you can go directly to a bar or a massage parlor where the girls are certainly "bad girls"; your basic problem will be negotiating a price after you pick one out. But another possibility is to go for a walk in the Park Central in the early evening or to a late-night disco and try to change a good girl into a bad one. Besides the promises of dinner, dancing, and a comfortable place to stay, one might throw in a day of shopping to complete the persuasion.

A word of warning though: sometimes you may not know whom you're dealing with. Some "bad girls" are very shy, some "good girls" aggressive. I once met a girl in a cafe in Brazil who went directly with me to my room, but when I offered money, she declined, saying it was "against her principles." Another time I met a beautiful accountant at Les Moustaches Disco in Costa Rica, and after a night of dancing and flirting I was convinced she was in love with me. Once in the room she demanded $100 (she thought I was in love with her), then made a quick exit when I de-

Key Largo Sweeties

clined her monetary demands. I was of course disappointed but learned a good lesson: not all prostitutes are "bad girls" (in some countries prostitution may be a girl's only means of support beyond low minimum wages); conversely, not all "good girls" are angels. Part of the fun of travel is figuring out which is which.

Key Largo is certainly the best bar in all of San Jose for American men. It's an old, colonial mansion, fully restored in the Casablanca style, a combination bar, disco, and restaurant, situated across from the Holiday Inn and Morazan Park (at Avenida 7, Calle 3), the perfect place to meet the bad, the good, and the in-between women. The charm is that you have no idea what type you are approaching.

If a girl sits down next to you and asks your name and what hotel you're staying at, she may be wanting to make a new friend, or she may be trying to find out if your hotel will accept her or if she will have to come up with a cheap room for the two of you. If you get to the point of negotiating a price for the night, the cost of a cheap room is included in her price. Remember, once, you buy her a drink, you are hers until you tell her to leave; no other woman will approach you. If she doesn't interest you after you've talked a little, simply tell her that your wife is waiting for you at your hotel. She'll disappear quickly. Since this is the classiest

Chapter 5

bar in San Jose, so are the prices: girls will start by asking for about $100; the later in the evening, the lower the prices go. Don't be afraid to negotiate, but only if you are truly interested. These girls don't like to be fooled with. Don't waste their time; just say politely, "I'm not interested."

In addition to being a good spot to find the obvious "working girls," Key Largo is also a great place to dance, browse, and flirt. Here you'll come across the amateur, who after a few dances and drinks can be persuaded. This is certainly the best place to begin your search.

Next door there are a few other interesting bars that, while not as big or sophisticated, can be lots of fun. These are great places to get to know your new partner from Key Largo in a more subdued environment. **Nashville South**, **Jazz Works**, and **Piano Blanco** are on Calles 7 or 5 below Key Largo (towards Paseo Colon). These small bars cater to specific musical tastes and have attentive hostesses. **Risa's** (Calle 1, Avenida Central) is crowded with yuppies and businessmen.

Before going on to the other interesting night spots, I should explain what sort of woman you can approach in Costa Rica: *anyone*. It's not like it is in the States where some women judge you by your build, your age, your clothes, or the kind of car you drive. In Costa Rica you are welcomed for your kindness and your non-macho attitude (the same goes for Thailand, Brazil, and the Dominican Republic). Being a strange man from a distant world is like having your Mercedes parked at the front door. In other words, don't be afraid to approach a 20-year-old model who looks like a goddess; you just might be her god. The rules here are different, so take advantage of them.

For the latest happenings, check with the **Tico Times**, which comes out on Fridays. If you can't find it at the bookstore next to the Gran Hotel, pay a cab driver to bring it to you (obviously pay him upon delivery). One of my favorite places to pass time and look for Miss Right is **Park Central**. Here is where everyone congregates in the early evening. Girls in mini-skirts who wink at you are exactly what you think they are. Sit on a bench, watch the world go by, and perhaps someone interesting will sit next to you. Don't be afraid to start a conversation, as most Costa Ricans speak a little English.

On the southwest corner of the park (Avenida 4, Calles 2 and 4) is the famous **Park Hotel**. If you haven't met anyone interesting yet, go on over for a drink. This American-owned hotel is the *poor-man's* Key Largo. Not only is the bar full of young ladies waiting to meet you but the hotel caters to your lusty needs by renting rooms by the hour. Admittedly the women aren't as classy as those in the bars on the other side of Paseo Colon, but then again, we're not talking about marriage, are we? This whole area is somewhat of a red-light district; the later it gets, the redder it gets. Check out the bars in the area, but do be careful: showy people have been known to get robbed. Also, the Park Hotel Bar is just a great place to kick back, listen to a few unbelievable stories from the old-timers, watch CNN, and flirt with the barmaids.

A last possibility is the UNI-SEX barber shops that dot this area. A good one is on Calle 6 between Avenidas 6 and 8. They really are barber shops, but upstairs you'll find a massage parlor where four or five girls are waiting for you. If there is someone who appeals to you, ask for the full treatment. If, however, you feel uncomfortable about being so direct, just take the massage and have the girl convince you that you need more. The cost is around $25. Watch out, though, for it can get a little seedy if you wander too far away from the park.

If you really want to fall in love, then go to a disco on a weekend. The problem, for me at least, is that they start very late (11:30 P.M.) and are so noisy that it's hard to get to know someone. The best American-style disco is **Les Moustaches,** at Centro Colon and Paseo Colon.

Outside of San Jose, the night is much tamer. The only area that comes close to being lusty fun is the bars of Puntarenas. During your travels away from the cities, you will meet Germans, Canadians, even a few Japanese. These fellow explorers are anxious to make new friends. Most everyone is curious as to what Americans are really like, and you can play this curiosity to your advantage. Of course, there are people who will do anything to avoid loud, showy Americans. So remember, wherever you are, you are an ambassador.

GETTING HOME

Just take a cab to the airport, which is only 20 minutes away from downtown San Jose. Arrive early, as the check-in is slow and confusing. Don't forget to reconfirm at least three days before your departure and tell them what hotel you are staying at, just in case the flight schedule changes.

Dominican Republic

One of the great mysteries of my travels is why more Americans don't travel to the Dominican Republic. The Europeans have discovered this lush, nearly tropical Caribbean island with fantastic accommodations, cheap food and entertainment, and crystal clear beaches only an hour and a half from Miami. If I were asked to name a refuge for the single male, I would have to say, the Dominican Republic. Granted, it doesn't have volcanoes, train tours through the jungle, exotic parks and animals, or a peaceful past, but it does have two international airports, a truly cosmopolitan city in Santo Domingo, a jewel of a beach resort to the north called Sosua, a windsurfing beach par excellence called Cabarete, a one-of-a-kind resort to the east in Casa de Campo, a club Med (if you must), and best of all, more gorgeous, available women than one knows what to do with. Don't let the crazy neighbor Haiti stop you from visiting one of the best kept secrets in the Caribbean.

The island of Hispaniola, which includes Haiti and the Dominican Republic, was founded by Christopher Columbus during his first voyage to the New World, becoming the first Spanish colony in the Americas. The Spanish influence is quite evident today.

The Dominican Republic has had a difficult history in this century. May 16, 1930 was the beginning of the dictatorial era of Trujillo who governed the country with an iron hand until his assassination on May 30, 1961. During his reign, there were advances in medicine, education, and communication, but the extravagances of his family were legendary, for not only did they rape and plunder the country but through torture they established a climate of fear, making the people very resentful. Almost all the large businesses were his family's and his racist policies culminated in a Haitian massacre in 1937. He believed that life in his country would be better if there were more whites, so he opened the door to European immigration. All European nationalities were represented, including many Jewish refugees who settled in a small town on the north coast which now is one of the most unusual and beautiful resorts in the Caribbean -Sosua.

When Trujillo died, he had a person worth of more than $200 million, but his country was decaying. Four years later, Lyndon Johnson sent in U. S. troops to restore order. Even now there is some political instability, but the new government is aware that foreign tourism is their most important industry, and essential to their successful operation in the modern financial world.

Its bloody past and uncertain political climate haven't stopped the Europeans from coming to the Dominican Republic and it shouldn't stop you. This country is determined to make itself a world-class destination, and you should get there before it's spoiled by rampant development.

GETTING THERE

There are three main airlines connecting the Dominican Republic with the United States. The local carrier, Dominicana de Aviacion, has flights from New York and Miami. (809-532-8511: note that you can direct dial the Dominican Republic just as you dial any other area code in the U.S.) American Airlines, (800-437-7300) also offers a similar service and Continental (800-231-0856) has connecting service through Newark, N. J. Since each of these airlines flies to Puerto Plata, it makes sense to see which will give you an open-jaws ticket for the price of a round trip. For example, on my last trip I flew into Santo Domingo, took the bus (their first-class buses are like airplanes) to the north coast where Puerto Plata, Sosua, Playa Dorada and Cabarete are, and flew home from the small and friendly international airport at Puerto Plata. This approach allowed me to see quite a bit of the country in only a week.

Another choice is to first fly to San Juan, Puerto Rico. This is a Caribbean hub for American Airlines, which has continuing service to the Dominican Republic. Delta and U.S Air also fly to San Juan, which from the west coast is sometimes cheaper than if you are using an east coast hub. The 40-minute flight to Santo Domingo is currently only slightly more than $100.00 roundtrip on American Airlines or Dominicana Air. If you do it this way, you have a great opportunity to see two fun cities for the price of one.

CLIMATE

A warm, tropical climate is predominant in the coastal areas. The average temperature is 77 degrees Fahrenheit, with January being the coolest month, and August the warmest. There are two main rainy seasons: the longest is from May to August, with a lighter season in November and December. The southwest (where you will find Casa de Campo) is the driest of the regions. I've been in Santo Domingo in the middle of May when it rained every day, but on my last trip, during the middle of April, I never saw a cloud. By the way, April 15 is usually when the hotels go to summer rates and 50% discounts are common.

Chapter 6

BASIC BACKGROUND INFORMATION

The Dominican Republic is the second largest island in the Greater Antilles, second only to Cuba. Spanish is the official language, but English is widely spoken, and everyone seems to have a relative in Miami or New York. Taxis are the main transportation for the tourist, but one interesting difference is that all major hotels have their own taxis, so if you find a driver you like (no one knows a city or its lusty prospects better than a taxi driver) you can always ask for him. This is a good idea since some stops require a driver waiting for you, and having someone you know makes for fewer problems.

Note also that restaurants add a 10% service charge automatically, and hotels add 5% to the room rate plus a 6% consumption tax. You are also taxed on both entering and leaving the country ($10 a stop for the so-called tourist card)! The electric current is the same as ours, 120 volts. If you don't have a passport, you'll need some proof of citizenship, such as a birth certificate.

The unit of currency is the peso, and the law states that all foreign exchange must take place at a legally-established center. This means that without your receipt from your exchange, no one will give you dollars for pesos when you leave the country. Since only a small difference exists on the black market (whereas in Brazil the difference can be 30% or more), it's wise to change your dollars at your hotel or bank. I found the many casinos around the tourist hotels to be the best legal place to exchange currency.

The Dominican Republic now has a toll-free travel hotline with information on sightseeing, beaches, transportation, currency, etc. Call 800-752-1151 from 8:00 A.M to 5:00 P.M. EST.

WHERE TO STAY IN THE CAPITAL: SANTO DOMINGO

Santo Domingo of the island of Hispaniola, is the first city of the Indies. Las Americas International airport is only thirty minutes east of the capital. Many people make Santo Domingo their starting point because of its central location.

Santo Domingo is a horizontal-spreading city that has been growing throughout the years and overflowing from its natural borders (the Ozama-Haina Rivers to the west and the Isabela River to the north) to become the largest Caribbean metropolis. The city is noisy, congested with traffic, and over populated. It is, however, reasonably safe and offers many activities and history lessons into our own past. The main business center is on the east end but it is not recommended to be there at night. Don't fret, for all the action moves to the beach boulevard, the Malecon, when the sun goes down. Every whim and all vices -gambling, drinking, and women - have the possibility of being realized.

As far as accomodations go in Santo Domingo, I recommend the following hotels. Remember rates drop by over 50% after April 15 until December.

Sheraton A beautiful high-rise on the Malecon, with casino, new pool, disco, and tennis courts. An American hang-out, the location and facilities make it an ideal home. All rooms have a view of the sea. (809-686-6666 or 800-325-3535)

Hotel Santo Domingo This is a gracious, old, tropical, elegant city landmark on the west side of the Malecon, away from the craziness of the street. The interiors were done by the contemporary Dominican architect Oscar de la Renta.

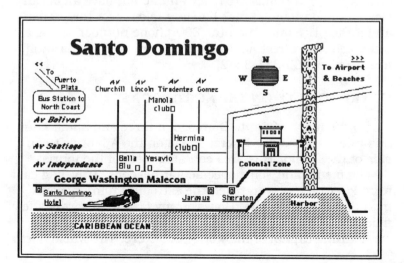

Quiet and respectable, this hotel offers a beautiful pool, gardens, a tennis club, the world-famous **El Alcazar** restaurant, the elegant Las Palmas night-club, and a 66-room executive floor. Rates include a secretary. This an excellent place to bring a new friend, not to find one. (800-223-6620)

Hotel Hispaniola This is the sister hotel of the Santo Domingo, situated directly behind her. It's not as classy or expensive or fussy about whom you bring in, but you can still use all the facilities of the Santo Domingo. A nice touch is the waiting lounge at Las Americas International Airport with mini-buses that bring you to and from your hotel. (800-223-6620)

Gran Hotel Lina This is the perfect medium-priced hotel (under $100 even in high season) with 220 rooms, 60 with an ocean view. Nice pool, casino, and a great piano bar. (800-223-6764)

Jaragua Hotel and Casino This is my choice for the place to be. Situated on the Malecon and next to the Sheraton, the Jaragua has six restaurants, five cocktail lounges, marble bathrooms with televisions, computerized door locks, the largest casino in the country, an Olympic-size pool amidst 14 acres of gardens, a European spa, clay tennis courts and the only New York deli in Santo Domingo. The lobby and casino are perfect for people watching. The cheaper garden rooms are noisy and do not have an ocean view. Ramada Renaissance has just taken over the property and if the price quoted on the 800-phone number seems a little high, call direct. (809-221-2222 or call Ramada's toll free number 800-331-3542)

WHERE TO STAY ON THE NORTH COAST

To the north of Santo Domingo, a three and a half hour bus ride, is the fabled **Puerto Plata** on the Atlantic Ocean side of the island. This area contains most of the tourist developments and some spectacular beaches. Traveling east from Puerto Plata, you reach the extremely touristy compound of **Playa Dorada**. However, my favorite resort is a few miles more, **Sosua,** and a little farther comes the windsurfing capital of the world, **Cabarete**. The whole north coast is one long beach full of quaint inns, large hotels and camp grounds. Many Canadians and Europeans make this area their winter home.

Playa Dorada

This is a complex of five hotels situated around a beautiful golf course in a gated, beach community. All the properties have time-share arrangements. Its casino, restaurants, bars, and beach are ten minutes east of Puerto Plata. The only problem is that you won't find any Dominicans here, only Canadians and other tourists. In fact, if you meet a new love in Puerto Plata, you have to sneak her in. I don't see why a single male would want to stay here, but if you must, then I'd suggest the following:

Eurotel right on the beach with 400 modern rooms and suites, with rock gardens and a great restaurant. (809-567-5159)

Playa Dorada Hotel formerly the Holiday Inn, this hotel, also right on the beach, is where you find non-stop action with casino and disco. (809-562-2774)

Princess Hotel A short walk to the beach, this hotel, formerly the Radisson, features four-plex apartments for comfortable living and a tennis center. (800-628-2216)

Some of these hotels have evening buffets and local entertainment (fashion shows, etc) to create crowds to keep their fun reputation. The golf course is superior and a running or biking boardwalk surrounds the greens with lakes and waterfalls to keep you cool. A new shopping center makes this complex so complete you never have to leave, unless you are looking for local women. But with all the beautiful beaches in the Dominican Republic I don't understand why they would build such a development on such a average beach when only a few miles east the water turns crystal clear and the sands are golden!

Sosua

This village with chic boutiques, little restaurants, bars, and discos is the perfect vacation spot for the single male who likes to watch people. It reminds me of Buzio's, the little village outside of Rio that Brigitte Bardot made famous. Sosua is as close as you'll come in the western hemisphere to the French Riviera: lots of **topless and G-stringed girls** on one of the best beaches in the Caribbean. Since it's only five minutes to the Puerto Plata airport, you don't even need a car. Here's a list of recommended accomodations:

Sosua Paradise Resort, (809-571-3438) and **One Ocean Place,** (809-571-2360) both have their own private beach within walking distance of the action.

Sosua by the Sea, (809-571-3222 or fax 571-3020), is an up-scale hotel overlooking the beach, whereas **Woody's** is the in-town choice (809-571-2032).

Sand Castle Resort is a world apart, or as their advertisements say, romantic and beautiful. Situated on a cliff overlooking the Puerto Chiquito beach, it is without a doubt the place to stay, a few miles by shuttle bus from crazy Sosua and three miles east of the airport. Time share units are available and this is one of the most beautiful resorts in all the Caribbean! (800-446-5963)

Colonia Sol y Mar is the perfect place to stay if the Sand Castle Resort next door is full. You can stay in a suite with a full kitchen and an ocean view for half the price. Who needs air-conditioning when you've got the sea breeze? (809-571-3250)

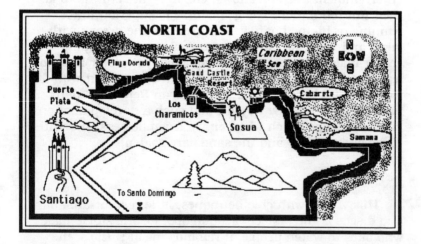

Bommarito Realty is the largest realty company on the north coast with the nicest condos and homes in the area and will be more than happy to do all your bookings for you. If you stay more than a week, you get a special discount. (809-571-2604 or fax 809-571-2406)

WHERE TO STAY ON THE SOUTHEAST COAST

To the southeast of Santo Domingo is Costa Caribe which includes the beach resorts of **Boca Chica** and **Juan Dolio**. A little farther is the magnificent **Casa de Campo** resort. The beaches on the far end of this coast (**Macao to Punta Cana**) are truly beautiful with crystalline sand, palm and coconut groves, and all sorts of seafood. Three recently completed projects have transformed this once sleepy area into a new tourist destination with a newly designed international airport. Here you'll find the Bavaro Beach Hotel, Punta Cana Yacht Club and a flashy Club Med.

Casa de Campo one of the world's great resorts, an hour outside Santo Domingo and half an hour from the airport. If you like the idea of staying in the main city and spending just a few days on the beach, this is the place. Casa de Campo was created by Gulf & Western (the oil company) and now offers over 900 rooms and villas, fourteen swimming pools, seventeen tennis courts, two professionally-designed golf courses, an Altos de Chevon, art village, yachting, polo grounds and stables, marina, private airport, and 7,000 acres of tropical foliage. You get the idea. (800-223-6620)

Hamaca Beach Resort If Casa de Campo is a little too much for you, yet you still want only a few days away on the beach, a good choice is Hamaca Beach Resort. Situated at the popular beach of Boca Chica, only half an hour from Santo Domingo and a few minutes from the airport, this crystal-clear cove is packed on weekends and is full of little bars and restaurants. It's a great place to kick back and make new friends. The new hotel, with 256 Caribbean-view rooms, should be open by early 1993.

Chapter 6

Relaxing at Boca Chica

It should be obvious that the Dominican Republic has made a total commitment to the tourist trade. I have offered you only a sampling of hotels and places to explore. New projects are going up every day, but for some reason most of the advertising money goes to Europe.

TRANSPORTATION

There are three possibilities for your explorations of the Dominican Republic. First, spend a few days in Santo Domingo, then head off to the north coast by bus and rent a car in Puerto Plata (the drive to the north coast is confusing and there is a one-way drop-off charge for car rentals). Alternatively, land in Puerto Plata airport and rent a car to drive directly to Sosua. A third choice is to stay in Santo Domingo for most of your time (I guarantee you there is enough to keep you busy) and take a few days for sightseeing by car or taxi to the east coast beaches. Or consider **Metro Bus Service**. With two morning and two afternoon drives to Puerto Plata, this service is deluxe, on-time, with toilet and snack vendor on board (566-6587). Your front desk will make reservations for you.

If you are renting a car, I recommend Budget: Of all the car rental agencies you could spend an entire day calling, this seems to be the best, reasonably priced with offices at

Las Americas airport, Puerto Plata airport, Puerto Plata proper, and Santo Domingo. Their central reservation number (567-0175) makes it easy, but make sure you tell them the exact location where you want to pick up your car.

As for taxis, outside your hotel, it's taxi-cab heaven. Everyone has a cab, so make friends with one you like, spend some time getting to know the driver, test his English, and bargain with him for your longer jaunts. An excursion to Boca Chica is the perfect place to try him out if you don't want to drive. Remember, your hotel has a private fleet of taxis which are more expensive, but on short trips the difference is insignificant.

WHAT TO SEE AND DO

Santo Domingo, founded by Columbus's brother, Miguel, is one of the oldest cities in the western hemisphere. Several significant firsts for the Americas have taken place in Santo Domingo: **Saint Francis**, the oldest monastery in the New World (dating back to 1508); the site of the first archbishopric (established in 1510 and constructed in 1524); the first settlement to be granted a title by an archbishop; the first university (Santo Tomas de Aquino, in 1538); and one of the first hospitals in the western world. Walking around the waterfront is a real history lesson.

Some of the more interesting sights are the **National Botanical Gardens** (the largest in the Caribbean), the **Colonial Section** (dating back to 1502, this is one you should walk), the **Convent** (an impressive sixteenth-century building made of brick and tile), **Columbus Park** (where there is a huge statue to the great admiral), **Las Damas Street** (which legend says owes its name to the ladies of the court of Maria de Toledo), **Ozama Fortress** (the oldest stone military fortress in the Indies, on Las Damas St.), and the **Museum of the Royal Houses** (with its fascinating collection of weapons and galleons).

The most important sight though is the **Alcazar Palace** and its neighboring street, Atarazana, with its hidden bars, restaurants and shops. In colonial days the Alcazar was the Royal Arsenal, Warehouse, and Customs; now it's a great place to cool down and have a beer. At the end of the street is **Fonda of the Atarazana**, the perfect restaurant for a romantic dinner, which is very possible in this city where finding companions is quite easy.

To buy that unusual gift or just to browse, the place to go is **Calle El Conde**, where on one of the oldest pedestrian shopping streets in all the Americas you'll find leather shoes, gold and silver goods, local artifacts, and children's hand-embroidered clothing.

La Romana, only a few hours east of Santo Domingo and the airport, is probably the most internationally-known of the cities of the Dominican Republic, not for its history but for its urban development. It began as a sugar mill, but turned to tourism in 1970, due to falling sugar prices. Now it holds two of the country's main attractions: **Altos de Chevon** (a replica of the sixteenth-century Italian town, and known as the village of the artists) and of course the famous resort of Casa de Campo.

San Pedro de Macoris is a great town to take in a local baseball game. Why? Because half of the 300 or so Dominicans in the major and minor leagues in the U.S.A. are from this little town, including Tony Fernandez, Alfredo Griffin, Mariano Duncan, Jose Uribe, and Rafael Ramirez. Who knows whom you'll you see in the stands? More baseball scouts come to San Pedro than to any other city in the world.

Santiago is the second-most important city in the Dominican Republic, due to its tobacco and sugarcane industry. Since the bus to Puerto Plata stops here daily, you could get off for a day tour. Its women are said to be the most beautiful in the country. It's also the home of *Merengue*, the national rhythm. The manicured lawns and interesting nightlife could make this an enjoyable stop if you are not in a hurry.

In **Puerto Plata**, the main north coast beach town, you might stop by the fort (San Felipe) that dates back to the sixteenth century, or take an excursion to the national park reached by a 2,565-foot cable car, or waltz through the central park with gazebos and the art deco lines of the Church of San Felipe. At the park are small boys offering to guide you. Tip them well because they are used to generous tourists from the cruise ships. But if there is a cruise ship docked in the bay, don't do the usual tours. Instead, head to Long Beach, two miles east of the city, where you will find across the street a nice hotel, the Puerto Plata Beach Resort (586-4243) and a fun casino.

Sosua, an old Jewish settlement located ten miles from the city of Puerto Plata, is where you'll find beautiful beaches, magnificent hotels, unusual restaurants and bars, and of course some interesting temples. The beach at Sosua is divided into two distinct areas: El Batey, where most of the modern disco and boutiques are, and Charamicos, where the locals live and party all night long. This whole area has become a magnet for foreign tourism and investments, with time-shares galore. Another advantage of this truly unknown oasis is that the international airport is only five miles away.

Cabarete, only five miles east of Sosua, is the new and upcoming resort. Cabarete is what Sosua was like twenty years ago, and I recommend you see it before it turns into a mega-resort full of Europeans. Besides its natural beauty, it is rated as one of the ten best windsurfing spots in the world, and its three miles of straight beach are perfect for the jogger. An added attraction is a lagoon, where visitors enjoy rowing and bird watching. Try the Punta Goleta Beach Resort with 126 rooms on 100 acres, with a tropical lagoon as your backyard and a fantastic beach as your porch! (809-571-0700)

If exploring, hiking, bird watching, or just car cruising is your thing, then I strongly suggest the drive from Puerto Plata to

Chapter 6

Samana Penninsula. Tropical forests, intimate hotels on forgotten beaches, unforgettable roadside restaurants, and only one road (west to east) makes this an easy drive with the unexpected around every turn. Lots of young girls hitchhike and when the police stop you, don't fret, it is their way of getting a tip (policemen are so underpaid that its the custom to stop traffic for an extra token; they just smile at tourists and let them pass).

Samana Peninsula is famous for its lush vegetation and a turquoise bay surrounded by small islets. The town of Samana is interesting, as this is where an underground population of freed black slaves settled from the United States. In 1870, the peninsula was almost annexed by the United States because of the strategic importance of its natural and well located harbor, but the annexation fell 10 votes short in the U. S. Senate. Today it still is a romantic, tropical, and sleepy village yet to be devoured by large-scale tourist development. It owes its beauty to the excellent beaches bordering both its northern and southern coasts which are lined with coconut palms and clear shallow waters. The ultimate get-a-way is the Bahia Beach Resort. Situated on one of Samana's beautiful beaches, this property is gifted with nature's abundance. Included is an enticing pool and a yacht to take you across the bay to the palm-laced keys, the best being Cayo Levantado. What a perfect place to take a new love or just to be left alone! (809-685-6060)

WOMEN AND NIGHTLIFE IN SANTO DOMINGO

Other than Rio, I can't think of any other place in the world where there is such a varied nightlife as Santo Domingo's **Malecon**. This street, called George Washington Ave., is a sea-front boardwalk boulevard running westward almost twenty miles from the Colonial sector. Most of the main hotels are located on this street, which is the center of excitement, especially on weekend nights. During the day the Malecon is the perfect place to jog, walk, or eat lunch at an outdoor cafe.

In Santo Domingo the possibilities for satisfying lustful desires are endless. For that afternoon appetite, there are massage parlors, or better yet, **Casas de Familia**, which are boarding houses for ten to fifteen girls, who sit in a living room, giggle and wink at you as you sip a coke and try to decide if one of them is for you. If yes is the answer, it costs about $25, plus a tip, depending on your enjoyment. You cannot take these girls out, but usually the upstairs bedroom and shower are clean. Again, your friendly taxi driver is your guide. Get to know him, for his trust and information are invaluable. Have him wait for you (you'll feel more comfortable knowing your ride home is right outside) and there is no extra charge since he gets a kickback if you decide to go upstairs.

My favorite evening entertainment is walking the Malecon after dinner. Here you'll be approached by cab drivers guaranteeing you the world, kids offering to be your guide, touts (a street hawker who for a price can find you anything or anyone) promising cheap hotel rooms, and girls trying to entice you.

A word of warning: if you are not interested, don't lead them on. These women will follow you for miles if they think you are bashful but interested. If one does appeal to you, spend some time with her, buy her a coke or a hotdog, and get to know what she is about. Some of these girls work and live in one of the Casas de Familia and it's just their day off. Others are simply trying to support their families; it's not uncommon for pregnant women to approach you. If your buddy, the cab driver, sees you talking to a street girl, he will probably yell at her, trying to scare her off, promising you that he knows of a better place. This scene can be quite entertaining. If you do decide on one of the Malecon cruisers, your next problem is where to take her, for you will have difficulty getting her to your room if she is not dressed properly. Of course these girls come up with their own solutions, but let me tell you, some of their suggestions even made me blush!

A third means of gratification are the upscale lounges and bars designed for your personal, intimate attention. The best are:

Chapter 6

Le Petit Chateau, a seaside, adult-entertainment complex, where not all the activity is on-stage and girls mill around, trying to make new friends. It's out on the far fringes of the Malecon, on Autopista 30.

Herminia Night Club, a well-known, lusty place to dance and eat creole food, where the girls won't bother you unless you look lonely or shy. It's located at Felix Evaristo Mejia and Esq. Maximo Gomez.

Manolo Piano Bar, more direct and to the point, "where you'll find young, attractive and cheerful girls," as their motto says. Your friendly cab driver waits for you (to make sure he gets his kickback from the management) while you go inside and have a drink. The girls are beautiful and dressed as if they were going to a prom. If someone interests you, just ask her to sit with you and buy her a drink. In this bar the management handles the girls, so all prices are established and there is no haggling. (In other lounges the girls are more freelance and set their prices depending on how wealthy you look). If you stay at Manolo's and use the upstairs facilities, it's around $45; double that amount and you can take her home for the entire evening. If you really hit it off with her, special deals are also possible for the rest of your stay. Dominican women are possessive and don't want to share a good man.

Le Petit Chateau, Stripper

Of course, there are also the discos and clubs which are a better source of beautiful women, but there are no guaranteed results. At these clubs, you really should listen to some **Merengue**, their national folk rhythm. Some of the best places to sit, listen, dance, or just people-watch are as follows:

Babilon Club, the largest and most luxurious disco in Santo Domingo, located on the Malecon (1005 George Washington);

Bella Blu Disco, one of the hot spots on the Malecon, stylish with plenty of Merengue and an uppity atmosphere, next door to Vesuvio;

Vesuvio, an exclusive restaurant and adjoining disco. Outside or inside, this is the perfect place to sit and watch the world walk by (521 George Washington; for reservations, call 689-2141);

Guacara Taina, a beautiful amphitheater, disco and restaurant located in real caverns (Mirador Park, 530-2666);

Merengue Lounge, located in the Jaragua resort and casino, with plenty of local entertainment, including the parading ladies;

Raffle's Pub, the bohemian, avant-garde bar of Santo Domingo, where you'll hear Reggae as hard rock with a little bit of blues. Located in the Colonial zone, right in front of the Saint Nicolas de Bari hospital ruins;

Chapter 6

No Lo Se, a place for the casual rendez-vous, with international music, drinks and snacks (corner of Maximo Gomez and Bolivar Avenue).

If you are a night person, Santo Domingo is for you. There are hundreds of bars, discos, and outdoor cafes to explore along with the beautiful women to meet. Remember, the night starts late, and if you show up at 10:30, you'll be solo but not for long.

WOMEN AND NIGHTLIFE ON THE NORTH COAST

Puerto Plata

This is a large, local town with a little of everything. The best place to meet, browse, eat and listen for interesting sounds is the central park around the picturesque gazebo. For entertainment, the disco and casino at the Puerto Plata Beach Resort is fun (and they have a great buffet), but you won't find any locals there. The one special place in town where there are tourists, locals, and ladies of easy virtue is **Vivaldi Studios**, at Hermanas Mirabal Street, across from Long Beach and within walking distance of the casino. Not only is the restaurant good but the music includes all styles. Don't be bothered if the local girls dance with themselves and ignore you. Sooner or later they'll let you know if they are available.

Playa Dorado

I see no reason to go into the Campo unless you are staying there or want to be surrounded by tourists. The best place for entertainment is the Playa Dorado Hotel, with its new casino, nightly shows, and busy disco.

Sosua

This is the fun spot on the north coast. Because of its unusual mix of tourists and locals, the night life is exciting. The main street of Sosua, Dr. Alejo Martinez, is filled with small bars, discos, and jamming houses. Walking around is the best way to find your spot; I prefer one where I can watch the street action, for there is always something interesting walking by. The combination of German, British, and Swedish girls with the local women makes this little village something to behold in high-season: a fashion show in the style of the French Riviera!

The best disco is **Banana's**, one block south of the town center. Here the population from Los Charamicos and the tourists come together, and you'll find whatever you are looking for. If you get bored or lonely, a walk through nearby **Los Charamicos,** where the blacks and Dominicans live, will certainly make you an instant celebrity. Admittedly, it doesn't look like the safest of places, but there are so many people out listening to the music, smelling the aromas, looking at the broken cars in the front yards, and mini-skirted girls trying to outdo each other for your attention, I think you'll agree that Los Charamicos is not to be missed. Also there are some great local restaurants here.

Now let me describe what it's like on the gorgeous Sosua Beach. During the day you will be approached by all sorts of people selling their wares (from fruit drinks to hats to water-sport equipment to jewelry to dolls). Boys will approach you, wanting to be your guide. Ask one to bring you a drink and start up a conversation. During your talk he will offer his services for all your needs, and if he says he can bring you a girl, make sure to explain that his tip will come only if she is to your liking. When I travel, I sometimes try to see what I can get away with. I was astonished when my new friend brought back two girls for me to interview. They were nice, but not right for me, and so I spent an hour buying them lunch, tipped my guide for his effort, and explained to the girls that I wasn't in the mood but maybe another time. I had an enjoyable afternoon though as I love to browse and flirt until I find my sweetheart. This is the only beach I've ever been on that the girls are brought to me, and for the single male, considering the beauty of the beach and its people, Sosua is heaven. Be courteous even if you don't accept a lusty offer — and you will get propositioned throughout the day and during your evening stroll.

Chapter 6

Perhaps take one of the girls to lunch or dinner. Finding out how the other half lives is what independent travel is all about.

Adjacent to the main beach is a shopping and eating bazaar with fresh seafood restaurants, local handcrafts, and of course, a hundred tee-shirt shops. Don't forget that Sosua is divided into two distinct sectors, El Batey (the tourist section) and Los Charamicos. All the local girls live in the latter section and an early dinner will guarantee an evening companion. Remember, the discos don't start until after midnight so find a nice cafe to flirt, relax, and view the sidewalk parade.

GETTING HOME

Given the choice, I would depart from the international airport at Puerto Plata. It is quaint, peaceful and you can wait in the open-air lounge. All major airlines depart for the U.S. from here, and you'll also have no problem returning the car you rented. As I mentioned, if you still have Dominican pesos and no receipt, the bank won't change them back to dollars. Find a cab driver or a local employee and promise him a 20% tip if he converts them for you. He might even drive back to Sosua to find dollars for you while you wait at the airport. Of course there is another $10 departure tax to pay, and you wonder what happened to that $10 arrival tax that you already paid. As they say, they get you both coming and going.

Part 3
Far Away
and a
Lot More Fun

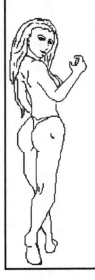

- **Brazil**

- **Bangkok**

- **Excursions in Thailand**

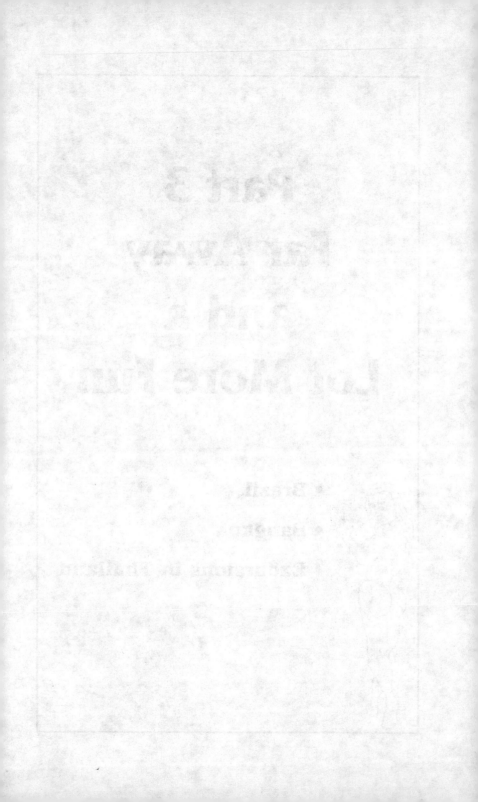

PICK A PARADISE: BRAZIL OR THAILAND

It may seem strange, but it's true; the farther away you get from the borders of the U.S., the more fun and exciting life gets. Two of the best travel destinations left for the single male are Brazil and Thailand. Yes, they are far away, the tickets are expensive, the languages are incomprehensible, the customs weird, and if you get sick or bored or just miss your cat, it will take more than a day to get home, but they are worth it.

Both countries may pose a culture clash that can be a little confusing or frustrating at first; like the endless wait for your bill in a Brazilian restaurant or the the nose rub on each cheek which constitutes the Thai kiss. But as dissimilar as one might think these two countries are, there are many surprising similarities that make both worlds true heavens for the single male. The most interesting is the abundance of females. Besides bars, massage parlors, discos, outdoor cafes, and even your hotel lobby, there are countless opportunities for one-night stands — which you pay for one way or another — or the prospects of truly falling in love with an exotic beauty. Other similarities besides their distance are warm climates, a scarcity of Americans, great local airlines for sightseeing, fantastic historic relics, regional foods, and a general laid back jeans-and-tennis-shoes atmosphere where almost anything goes.

In Brazil the women are not ashamed of their bodies and show as much as they can, be it on the beach, on the side-walk, or on the dance floor. Besides going topless on the beach, the Brazilian women will run, sing, flirt, drink, and dance you to death. Sometimes you'll wonder who is hustling whom. No place in the world has such beautiful, outgoing, and entertaining women who pray for a sunny day just to show off their bodies. In addition to beautiful bodies, Brazil has great cities, beaches, parks, sights, restaurants, and of course music. Here everyone works out and plays volleyball, and it's possible to spend an entire day and never take off your bathing suit.

Remember, going to Rio and saying you've been to Brazil is like going to Miami and saying you've seen the entire United States. Brazil is the size of our country, and has as many diverse cultures as all of Europe, and is truly fascinating to explore. An added bonus is the ease of jetlag-free, north-south travel.

On the other side of the world is Thailand, a 17-hour flight from Los Angeles with no non-stops but good connections through Japan, Korea, or Taiwan. Although women are aplenty — over 500,000 women in Bangkok alone are full- or part-time professionals — they aren't as visible as in Brazil. Thai women stay more within their female and Buddhist roles of polite, respectful homebodies. This country is smaller than California and all destinations are within a two-hour flight; the capital city, Bangkok, has chaos, pollution, and horrendous traffic jams on a daily basis, but there is also mystery and intrigue around every corner. The women you'll meet will come from the bars, but none will be topless on the beach, or eye you in a cafe, or even acknowledge you on the street. Part of the Asian mystique is that the man makes all the moves and the women are content to stay in an air-conditioned room and watch television. However, at this time, there is a new feminist movement for more equality and job advancement due to Thailand's recent economic growth, which has led to a critical shortage of skilled labor.

Besides the image of a *night in Bangkok*, Thailand has much to offer in great hotels, pristine beaches that rival the Caribbean, spicy and exotic foods, and a culture full of temples and ancient ruins. The people are genuinely kind, patient, and curious about Americans in a subdued sort of way. Here you'll find countless European and Arab tourists enjoying the spoils, many with a girl on each arm. What most Thai girls dream of, however, is falling in love with an American and moving to America to join their friends.

Both Brazil and Thailand have the best to offer in entertainment, sights, reasonable prices, and the feeling that you're really on an adventure. After spending the summer in Europe, I ask myself, why waste time in countries where I'm just another tourist when I could be in Brazil or Thailand living royally but at half the price. I guess the question is like "why do men climb unknown mountains?" *Just to see what is on the other side and reinforce their knowledge that the valley they are in is the best.* Brazil and Thailand are the best.

Brazil

Brazil is almost the size of the United States. It is the fifth largest country in the world and has the eighth largest population, about 150 million, most of whom are scattered around the coastal area. Many South Americans think of the Brazilian as a separate race since they look, act, and eat differently.

However, the opposite is true; the Brazilians are among the most ethnically diverse people in the world: original Indians, European immigrants, African slaves — truly a racial mix. Soon after the Portuguese discovery of Brazil by Pedro Cabral in the early 1500s, slaves were brought over from Africa, and the mixing of the European Catholicism and African Macumba began a new culture and a hybrid religion, evident today in Samba rituals and during carnival time.

Today, the people called *cariocas* are considered some of the friendliest people in the world. Perhaps the reason for their openness is the beautiful racial and cultural mix. This intermingling leads to surprises and excitement at any moment.

Brazil has one of the ten largest economies and is still growing. You might think of the country as only a strange land where they have good soccer players, tonga-clad beauties (a tonga is the little thread on the bathing suit for the woman's behind), crazy samba dancing, coffee, and nuts. But in reality, Brazil has much more to offer: Sao Paulo with a strong Japanese influence, the third-largest city in the world; Rio with its famous beaches of Ipanema and Copacabana; Manus, a duty-free port in the middle of the Amazon (Belem, on the mouth of the river, is even more interesting); Brasilia, a capital city built from scratch in the middle of nowhere, an architectural eighth wonder of the world; and Bahia (Salvador), with its voodoo churches and exotic foods and music, probably the most interesting city in all of Brazil.

There are 23 states in the country, and understanding the regionalism is an essential part of understanding Brazil. The north, which contains 42% of the land area, has great rain forests that supply the world with 20% of its water and 10% of all animal species. One can't tear down the rain forests and build towns and roads at will. This area is inhabited by the poorest of all Brazilian people, the Indians.

On the east coast are the cities of Rio, Recife, and Bahia, infamous for its slave heritage. Below Rio are the wealthy European-heritage cities of Santos, Curitaba and Porto Alegre. The capital Brasilia in the center of the country while the working capital, Sao Paulo, is a short thirty-minute shuttle flight north of Rio.

The new Brazilian president, Jose Sarney, now governs the 23 states in a democratic manner, but the military keeps a watchful eye especially on inflation, on the social conditions of the poor, and of course on the effects of tourism on the belittled economy.

The good news is that this country is still a hidden paradise, visited mostly by Europeans. Brazilians have tremendous curiosity about Americans and will bend over backwards to show off their country. If you can imagine a Black-Indian-Italian female mixture, called a *mulatto*, walking down the boardwalk in a tonga suit, and her only goal is to look good, then you get the picture. The national hedonism of the beach culture, tantalizing music and food, and one of the most relaxed attitudes towards sex in all the world make a trip to Brazil synonymous with heaven.

A SHORT HISTORY

In 1500, while looking for India, the Portuguese explorer Pedro Cabral discovered Brazil. Three decades later, the Portuguese king Joao III sent the first Portuguese to settle in Brazil. After the colonists discovered sugar cane's fantastic growth potential, the capture and sale of the African slaves became Brazil's second industry.

The Dutch invaded Recife in 1630, and the French landed in Rio in 1710. The country expanded quickly with European immigrants who were excited by the possibility of owning their slaves, becoming wealthy, and not having to work. At the time conditions in Europe were horrible (wars, disease, poverty) and anywhere must have sounded better. The multicultural mix in Brazil is quite evident today, with the cooler southern cities mostly German, Italian, and French, while the warmer northern cities are mostly black. This dimension of Brazilian culture makes it immensely interesting for the world traveler.

Chapter 7

Concerning Rio, its discovery was actually a mistake. First seen around 1502 by Vespucci, who was inspecting Cabral's discoveries in the north, Rio was thought to be the mouth of a huge river (thus the name Rio) and not a bay. The French settled it, but in 1565 the Portuguese returned and after a two-year war took control. Due to its strategic location, it became Brazil's capital in 1763, but it really wasn't until the European immigration boom at the beginning of the twentieth century that Rio became a truly international city.

Unfortunately, bad publicity, crime, and pollution, have had an impact, reducing the million-plus tourists to just over 600,000 per year. But Rio recently raised $2 billion to clean itself up and prove to the world it has a new and better face. Because of the United Nations Conference on Environment and Development in June 1992, Rio cleaned and dredged Guanabara Bay, renovated the airport, created new freeways to the city center, placed new signs and installed better lighting for the beaches, purchased new vehicles and equipment for the police, and moved the beggars out of the main city squares.

CLIMATE

Remembering that the seasons below the equator are reversed, winter in Brazil is from June to August, and the area below Rio gets snow once in awhile. Rio during this period is like a Southern California climate, moderate (60 to 75 degrees) but too cold for the Brazilians. The summer season, from December to February, is when school is out and many Brazilians go on vacation. In the summer period, Rio gets very hot and humid with short rainy spells. The average number of rainy days for Rio in January is 13, whereas May and September have only 5.

Late January is my favorite time to go, for not only do you miss the high-season hotel prices and vacationing kids and the hordes of European tourists, but the weather is better. In the north, where it's always hot, September and October are some of the least rainy months too. If you go to the Amazon entrance of Belem, an old and fascinating city, you will be surprised to learn that the people set appointments by the precise time of daily afternoon showers. This is one of the wettest cites in the world but you'll certainly know "when" to carry an umbrella.

GETTING THERE

The good news is that going north to south from the U.S. to Brazil produces very little jet-lag. From Miami to Rio is about eight-and-a half hours, and from Los Angeles it's eleven to thirteen hours. There are a few non-stop, direct flights. Beware, however, of the so-called direct flights which get you there on the same plane but which make up to five stops on the way.

The bad news is that Brazil is one of the few countries in the world that require a VISA stamped in your passport, a royal pain in the ass. Most major cities in the U.S. have a consulate, and you can mail in your passport (which I don't like to do) with the proper payment and hopefully they'll mail it back in about ten days. You'll need two pictures, a visa application (which you can get from some travel agents) and a stamped self-addressed envelope.

The major Brazilian consulates are:

3810 Wilshire Blvd	630 Fifth Ave.
Suite 1500,	Suite 503/505
Los Angeles, CA 90010	New York, NY 10020
(213) 382-3133	(212) 757-3080

777 Brickell Ave.
Penthouse,
Miami, FL 33131
(305) 377-1734

To book your flight, you have several good choices. First is the national carrier, Varig Airlines, which has non-stop flights from Miami, New York, and Los Angeles. At this writing, they have a special rate that includes five nights in a hotel, transfers, and breakfast for under $1,000. Call 800-

468-2744 and ask for their tour desk. Varig also allows unlimited stop-overs on its regular fares, so seeing Lima or Panama City is possible! A new Brazilian carrier to the U.S. is TransBrazil, which flies from Orlando to Miami, then on to Rio and Sao Paulo. TransBrazil has new flights from New York and Washington to their hub in Brasilia. From this strategic center you can connect to the fourteen main Brazilian cities. (800-872-3153).

Also a new airline, VASP, has just started four non-stop flights weekly from Los Angeles to Sao Paulo and Manus with direct service from San Francisco and on to Rio. (800-732-VASP).   These carriers also sell air-passes for $440 that allow three weeks of travel with four stops and a home base. Unlike other national carriers (such as Iberia of Spain, which requires that you buy your overseas flight with them in order to get their air-pass), you can buy these vouchers separately and fly, for example, on American Airlines if you wish, as long as you purchase them in the U.S. before your trip. A good alternate are the U.S. carriers United Airlines (800-241-6522) or American Airlines (800-433-7300), which bought out the old Eastern routes. United has taken over Pan Am routes from Miami and New York, with daily departures. If you belong to these frequent-flyer clubs, then use them for the miles. Once when Pan Am was giving triple miles for flights, one trip to Rio gave me enough miles for a free trip to Europe. Watch your newspaper for low-season promotions.

A third option to Brazil is Japan Airlines (800-223-3663) which I consider one of the best in the world. On a non-stop, Los Angeles to Rio, I was amazed to find that the stewardesses cleaned the washroom after every single use, no matter what time it was. Their new routing flies non-stop L.A.X. to Sao Paulo (flight #064 leaves L. A. at 9.30 A. M.}, but you must connect to Rio. The good news is that there is shuttle service (no reservations needed and flights every 30 minutes) to **Santos Dumont Airport** that is much closer to the beaches and a real bonus if there is traffic since it is a much cheaper cab ride.

An often overlooked carrier is Aerolineas, Argentina's national airline, which flies non-stop Miami and New York to Rio. They are a highly recommended airline and the pride of their country (800-333-0276).

The price for tickets is roughly similar from one airline to another, with the only differences being some travel package discounts on the price of hotels, for instance. I recommend trying to shop for discount tickets at a consolidator. These offers are very legitimate but do have drawbacks. You can save about 30% on the face value of the tickets, but if your flight is delayed, the tickets are honored only on the carrier for which they were written. In other words, if you miss your flight, you might have to wait for that exact flight the next day regardless of the reason. Also there is no refund, and ticket reservations must be made thirty days in advance and must be paid for when the reservation is made. Usually frequent-flyer miles are credited for the discounted tickets, and upgrades are possible. Always pay with a credit card even if the consolidator offers a discount for cash—at least you'll have some recourse in case something unpredictable happens. Some of the best consolidators are:

Access Intn'l
250 W. 57th Street, # 511
New York, N.Y. 10107
800-333-7280

Intn'l Travel
P.O. Box 371
Tampa, Fl 33601
800-999-2606

Brazil Expert Tours
3810 Wilshire Blvd.
Suite 611
Los Angeles, CA. 90010
213-387-2111

Holiday Tours
3328 Wilshire Blvd.
Los Angeles, CA.
90010
213-380-6644

Brazil Vacation Center
16 W. 46th St., 2nd floor
New York, NY 10036
800-342-5746

Chapter 7

If you must have the lowest priced ticket and don't want to deal with consolidators then try **Aero Peru** or **Air Paraguay**. These airlines fly new aircraft but the routing might not be best!

In Brazil, always remember to reconfirm your return flight and give the airline your hotel address. While changing a reservation in Bahia (I wanted to stay an extra day) I lost my connecting flight to Rio once when my name disappeared from their computer. They said they couldn't reach me to reconfirm. I had to beg, lie, demand, and cry a little to get my seat back on the flight to Rio. If I had not made it, I would have had to buy a new, expensive one-way return to Los Angeles. Don't give Murphy's Law a chance to work.

BASIC BACKGROUND INFORMATION

Money

One of the first issues to know about before going to Brazil is money. In 1989 Brazil had 1800% inflation, the equivalent of more than 100% per month. This has an impact on your exchange.

There are three exchange rates: first, the official rate (the one that Brazilians have to use); next, the *dolar turismo* (the one used by banks and hotels); and last, the *paralelo rate* (the true black market rate).

When you come from the airport, don't use the airport bank: it's a rip-off. Get a cab and pay the driver in dollars; he'll love it and ask if you want to exchange more at his special rate just for you; don't accept. The best place to exchange money is at travel agent offices where they likely offer the black market rate. Doing it on the street is foolish because the last thing you want is people watching you change dollars. Exchange only what is necessary since it varies each day and you can benefit by waiting, and keep your dollars and traveler's checks in a safe deposit box at your hotel. Remember that two days later you might get 10% more for your money, so exchange slowly and carefully.

One last thing, when leaving Brazil, you will find that the bank won't change *cruzeiros* back to dollars unless you have a bank receipt (which you won't have since you'll be using the black market rate), so plan ahead. Don't get stuck with a lot of cruzeiros.

On January 1, 1992 the central bank of Brazil devalued the cruzeiro 17% in order to increase the ailing economy. This means that foreign visitor dollars will go much farther than before, making Brazil an even better bargain.

Crime

Tourism has dropped over 20% in the last few years due to publicity about muggings, thefts, and crime. The fact that in Brazil the poor and the rich live so close to each other and constantly intermingle makes crime almost inevitable. One-fourth of the people in Brazil live below the poverty level, and many children barely survive. Quite a few live in shanty towns called **Favelas,** which, believe it or not, are right above the Sheraton Hotel. Stay away from Favelas. You've got to remember, however, that all modern cities have crime. In Brazil, it's no different: if you walk down the street with a Rolex watch, alligator shoes, red socks with dress shoes, and a billfold hanging out, you will get robbed. When you go to the beach, bring only five dollars for drinks and a chair. When you go out at night, wear blue jeans and tennis shoes and blend in! Don't be a fool!

News and Information

The better hotels will carry *CNN*, and at the news stands you will find the *Herald Tribune* and the *Daily Post*. The *Rio Today*, a once-a-week local English paper, also contains the latest happenings. Note also that Rio time is two hours ahead of Eastern time.

Food

First, don't drink the water; instead try the local mineral water, which is excellent. I like it with *gas*, a sort of a bubbly tonic. My favorite drink is *Guarana*, a delicious sugar fruit drink that is almost addictive. If there is such a thing as a national dish, *Feijoada* is it, and if you like spicy meat stew, you'll like this. If you are a big eater, the *Churrascarias* are for you. For a set price, they keep bringing you meat choices on spits until you beg them to stop. It's worth it to starve throughout the day just for this experience. Some up-scale restaurants will charge you a "*couvert*", or a price for fancy bread and its coverings; if you don't want it, just tell your waiter and you won't have to pay for it.

The Brazilian coffee is the best and strongest in the world. They bring it to you in small cups with sugar; it is meant to be drunk quickly.

As for washrooms, all hotels and restaurants have facilities that are available to the public. If you are on the beach and need a restroom, just walk to the nearest outside cafe.

Phones

The international code for Brazil is 55, and for Rio, 21. International collect calls are 000333; the operator is 000111; the U.S. country code is 1. The public phones on the street take tokens and usually don't work. If your hotel charges too much, there are Posto Telefonica offices for special calls.

Transportation

Most all your travels will be done by taxi, since it's not worthwhile to rent a car. The taxis are cheap, numerous, and fairly reliable. When going to new places, always ask for the fare and bargain a little if it's a major distance (it never hurts to try). Renting a car is possible, but finding your way around may be hard; even my tour driver to the nearby city of Buzios couldn't figure the way out of Rio! Leave the driving to someone else, and whatever you do, don't tell the driver that you're in a hurry. When a policeman gives you a "thumbs up" sign, he is asking if you are all right. The correct answer is to return a thumbs up, unless of course you do have a problem in which case, obviously, signal with thumbs down. If you're traveling after 11:00 P.M., there is a 40% surcharge in taxis, but it's worth it as you shouldn't walk alone late at night or in unknown areas.

Taxis in front of your hotel are bigger and more reliable, and some have air-conditioning, if you can convince the cab driver to turn it on. The ones on the street are much cheaper, and you can bargain easily. I guess it's just a case of your mood and the distance.

THE GEOGRAPHY OF RIO

Rio de Janeiro has been called the "cidade maravilosa," or the wonderful city. Situated on the southern shore of a harbor in beautiful Guanabara Bay, and stretching south-east twelve miles from the sea to the jungle mountains, Rio is indeed stunning. Over ten million people live in this city of 23 beaches, which start at the international airport on the north side of town, and proceed to Barra de Tijuca, the farthest beach to the south and 15 miles in length. The most famous, of course, are Copacabana, Ipanema, and Leme, on which you can spend 95% of your time playing in the sand, flirting in the cafes, and drinking and dancing in the neighboring bars and nightclubs. By the way, the French word *"boite"* is the name for the lusty type of night-club.

Modern Rio is divided into two basic areas — *Zona Norte* (northern) and *Zona Sul* (southern). Downtown, which is in the northern section, is just called *Centro*. This older area is commercial and noisy, typical of most modern cities. As you drive south through the neighborhoods towards the beaches, the roads are connected by impressive tunnels through the mountains. The famous beach areas are bordered by two mountains— Sugar Loaf, in the Botafogo area, and Corcovado, with its immense statue of Christ.

As you leave the first beach area called Flamengo (not worth visiting) you are on Ave. Princesa Isabel heading towards the renowned Leme, Copacabana, and Ipanema. Now is when your heart will throb as you're finally at the beach that invented the bikini, and the bronzed, tonga-clad women are everywhere. Yes, this is heaven.

RIO BEACHES

Ipanema

To Sheraton
>>>

Arpoador

Hotel
Caesar Park

Av. Vierra Souto

Rue Visconde de Morasis

Marina
Hotel

Av Mitre

Nabuco

Hippie
Fair

Rue Visconde Piraja

Hotel
Rio Palace

Night Bazaar

Hotel
Othon

Help
Disco

Barata Ribeiro

Atlantic

Copacabana Av

Copacabana

park
Av

Siaqueira Campos st

Apart
Hotel

Copacabana
Palace Hotel

Atlantic Suite Hotel

Late nite Cafes

Ronald

Belfort Roxo

Prado Jr

Carvalho st

Schervada Bar

Barberella Bar

Princess Isabel st

Leme

Sugar
Loaf

Rio Sul
Shopping
Center

Botafogo

Hotel Gloria

The Beaches of Rio

RIO'S AIRPORT

You'll arrive at the international airport of **Galeao** (there is another airport closer to the city called Santos Dumont which is used mainly for shuttle service to Sao Paulo). Once through immigration, after you've had your visa stamp and passport approved and gotten your luggage, there's a guard controlling a red light/green light as he checks people. Hopefully you'll get a green, allowing you to proceed directly to the arrival lobby. The red light is mainly for Brazilians re-entering, whose purchases abroad must be checked.

(If you have the unfortunate luck of forgetting to get a visa before entering the country, it's likely that they will make you get back on a plane and go to Argentina where you can enter the country without a visa. Don't fret. It's just a few hours flight, and when you arrive, you can simply go to the Brazilian consulate in Buenos Aires, and get your visa there.)

As you approach Rio from the north, the Centro appears first and you might be able to spot **Praca Mahatma Gandhi** (the main square) and **Cinelandia** (the movie area). This whole area, generally deserted by tourists who are all on the southern beaches, is actually lots of fun and a good place to see Brazilians at play.

As you drive towards the bay and pass Flamengo Beach on your left, the awesome grandeur of Rio becomes apparent. One more tunnel and you reach Leme, where Avenue Atlantica starts and your fantasy begins.

WHERE TO STAY IN RIO

Most of the tourist hotels are located in Copacabana and Ipanema. For a first stay, I would recommend a hotel in Copacabana where most of the entertainment takes place. If you want to be beyond Leblon, which is at the end of Ipanema, you can choose from the Intercontinental, the Sheraton, and the Nacional hotels, all of which are nice but are too removed from the people and the action. Who wants to come to Rio and lie on a private beach (like the Sheraton's) and see only Americans trying to hide from the Favelas above them?

Chapter 7

The majority of Rio's hotels are old and make the choices limited. I suggest staying in a five-star facility, for anything less could be a big disappointment. From north to south, my favorites are:

Meridian This fine French hotel chain contributes to the popularity of the beach atmosphere; on New Year's Eve, this 37-story landmark turns itself into a Roman candle and you know it's midnight. The hotel occupies an envious position where Ave. Princesa Isabel intersects the beach. Copacabana's red-light district is also right across the street. Ave. Atlantica 1020. (800-543-4300)

Ouro Verde Because it doesn't have a pool, this refined hotel is rated only four stars. This is probably the finest small hotel in Rio, with 66 rooms, some of which overlook the beach. Also has an excellent restaurant. Ave. Atlantica 1465; telex 23848.

Copacabana Palace This used to be the best hotel in Rio. Recently remodeled, with a fine pool and sunning terrace, it's still my favorite. Reminiscent of the Hotel Del Coronado in San Diego or the Don CeSar in St. Petersburg, Florida, this grand hotel with its fourteen-foot ceiling in the lobby and its own Teatro is one of a kind. Ask for a room in the Annex, not facing the beach, and you'll get an old-time apartment, a room the size of a house. The huge annex rooms not facing the beach go for the same price as the main hotel rooms, and if you can afford it, go for the annex ocean-facing rooms, which are like having an ocean-front condominium. ($150 and up!) Ave. Atlantica 1702. (telex 22248 or phone 257-1818)

Rio Atlantica Suite Hotel One of the few new hotels in Rio. I think this was a new apartment building they couldn't sell, so they turned it into a hotel. Its lobby and pool are small, but the ocean-front suites are now the choicest and most modern rooms on Copacabana. Ave. Atlantica 2964; (255-6332)

Othon Palace The major large tourist hotel in the area with over 600 rooms on thirty floors and a roof-top pool. Overrun with European tourists in high season, it's a good choice in shoulder season. I like its location — almost the middle of the beach and next to the largest disco, **Help**, in

South America and very popular with the ladies. The cafe in front is also very fashionable and lots of fun, especially late at night. Ave. Atlantica 3264. (telex 22655 or phone 255-8812)

Rio Palace A true luxury hotel at the south end of Copacabana and minutes to wonderful Ipanema. Two pools, one for morning sun and another for the afternoon — my kind of place! Besides elegance in the true Brazilian tradition, with rooms decorated in hardwood, tiles and marble, there is an 180-unit shopping center, Casino Atlantica, adjacent to the hotel. Ave. 4240 Atlantica. (phone 521-3232 or Telex 21803)

Aparta Hotel Copacabana This is an ideal solution for long stays, since it's an apartment building converted into hotel. This property, three blocks from the beach, is a great place to stay to get to know Rio. When renting a room on the beachfront, you really don't get a feel for a city; here you will. One or two-bedroom units are available, but the two-bedroom penthouses with their own whirlpool and ocean views will still cost less than an ocean-front hotel (currently less than $100/day if you take it for a week or more). Many fancy hotels won't let you take strangers to your room, and if they do allow night visitors, they might charge you "double occupancy" if she stays the entire evening. Here there is no one to tell you what to do. Use your imagination with what you could do with that extra bedroom in the pent-house.

Another interesting feature is a shopping center next door that has a massage parlor on the second level that caters to the Brazilian businessman, not to tourists. Of course they are more than happy to take care of your pressing needs; dollars are always preferred. Once you know a lady by her first name and the management knows you, house calls are allowed, a major advantage when you are in a hurry or feel lazy. There is an extra charge for this service, but you only live once. The hotel is on the corner of Siqueira Campos and Barata Ribiero, in an interesting residential area. You rent from an Imobiliaria (real-estate

Chapter 7

Copacabana Beach

company) that specializes in this property. Realty Apart
Hotel Imobiliaria LTD, 22040 Rio de Janeiro, Brazil or P.O.
Box 12.350 cep: 220222; (phone 021-235-5894; telex
388192 HSSN Br)

Caesar Park Hotel Ipanema has one truly outstanding
hotel, a little plush for me, but the Caesar Park is certainly
one of the best hotels in all Brazil with 230 rooms on 23
floors. If you bring your binoculars, you won't have to go to
a topless bar to see young ladies undress, for you are in the
middle of the best part of Ipanema beach. I must warn you,
though; it's expensive ($150+ per night). Ave. Vieira Souta
460. (287-3122)

THE BEACHES OF RIO

The beaches are what make Rio so special. Nowhere else in the world will you see business deals being consummated next to lovers or football games with topless cheerleaders. Life is on the beach; nothing else is important!

A few years ago I was to meet a friend in Rio who arrived a day before me. Having heard the exotic and lusty stories about Rio, and being recently divorced and hot, he got off the plane and immediately went to check out the topless prey. He spent hours walking up and down the beach drooling over the beautiful girls, but none seemed to be interested in him. He took off his shirt to show his weightlifter's physique, but still no response. When I met him that evening, he was thoroughly disappointed and said that Rio was just an exaggerated hype to get tourists. What he didn't understand was that the beach is actually a social institution; it a place to meet your friends, show off your new tonga, or check out the guys in the soccer game. I explained to him that the scene will change, that these girls who wouldn't give him a second look during the day will be winking at him at night. Unfortunately, he was so sunburned from his initial jaunt on the beach that no one could touch him for three days.

The first beach you'll want to check out is **Copacabana**, one of the world's most densely populated areas, practically a city within the city. It's only three blocks deep, so finding one's direction is easy. Here are the large hotels, numerous cafes along Avenue Atlantica, the three-mile-long mosaic boardwalk (the one you see in all the pictures) which is great for early morning runs and plenty of nightlife.

On weekends, the boardwalk gets very crowded, and so I suggest renting a chair on beach days; it's more comfortable and you'll have someone to watch your possessions (the same attendant is there every day and he'll get to know you by name). Once in Recife I fell asleep on the beach and someone stole my pouch, money, and tee-shirt from underneath me. I learned the hard way: don't bring anything valuable to the beach. With the young kids selling sandwiches and drinks, machos in their speedos searching for

Chapter 7

Miss Perfect, and a countless parade of beautiful women, this is an all-day carnival and you are likely to be easily distracted.

The next beach over, a long walk or short cab ride away, is **Ipanema**. This is where the song "the Girl from Ipanema" originated and is more fashionable, more expensive, and with a younger crowd than Copacabana. Ipanema has many upscale apartments facing the main street, Avenue Vieira Souta, and the beach ends in a residential area called **Leblon**, where there aren't many hotels or restaurants, but the classy discos and jazz bars make for great entertainment.

Next comes the area of **Vidigal**, but the only thing here is the **Rio Sheraton** and its private beach. If hang-gliding is your thing, the next beach of **Sao Conrado** (**Nacional** and **Intercontinental** hotels are here) is famous for its landing platform. The take off point is from Pedra Bonita, the mountain above. Another twenty minutes or so brings you to **Barra da Tijuca**, a new commercial and residential area for the wealthy. Here is the best place to rent a deluxe condo, not to mention **Barra Shopping**, the largest shopping mall in Rio. This area is also famous for its laid-back jazz and samba clubs, but you are a good thirty minutes away from Copacabana where the real action is. I would say that Barra da Tijuca makes for a good day-trip just to see how the other half lives.

Speaking of the other half, don't be tempted to go to the **Favelas** (shanty towns on the hill where the poor live) no matter what the cab driver promises you or how cheaply something is priced. If you must get "high" on something besides alcohol or beautiful women, pay the extra price and have it brought to you. Don't be foolish.

WHAT TO SEE AND DO IN RIO

The main event in Rio is Rio itself, but there are some noteworthy sights, the more interesting being:

Sugar Loaf The most famous and photographed sight in Rio. A cable car takes you up in two stages; first you land, after a 700-foot ride up, at Morro da Urca peak where you can visit a museum, or go to a disco and restaurants. At night the disco is beautiful, and during carnival they have a great ball and celebration. Urca gives a good view of Guanabara Bay, but from atop Sugar Loaf you can see all of the beaches. You get there by taking the second cable-car, which goes almost 800 feet straight up (if high altitude is not your thing, don't go!). Take a cab to the base of the mountain. It's open from 8:00 A.M. to 10:00 P.M. but the disco stays open till 1:00 A.M.

Corcovado This is the mountain that houses the statue of Christ, the Redeemer. The mountain is over 2,000 feet high, towering over the city, and the statue is 120 feet high and over 1400 tons. Here you'll see Christ's arms outstretched (over 75 feet) as if to protect the city. If you are in a hurry, you can take a cab to the top, but the old railway, which began operating in 1884, is much more fun. Starting at 8:00 A.M., the train leaves every thirty minutes. I must warn you, however, about one small thing to consider. The first time I took this railway tour, by the time I got to the top, the fog and mist had rolled in. I couldn't see Christ's face or the fantastic view. Nor could I get a refund. So I took a cab back and returned on a clear day.

View from Corcovado

Chapter 7

Jardim Botanico I enjoyed this botanical garden more than Tijuca Forest (a natural rain forest atop the mountain) because of the amazing variety (over 5,000 types) of plants and trees, including the largest lily pads in the world. With Corcovado in the background, this is a great place to stroll with your new love and get to know her. Seemingly though, wherever I wander in this park, Christ watches my every move and makes me feel eerie with my lusty thoughts.

Bateau Mouche This is basically a boat tour of Guanabara Bay during which you see the little islands, bridges, and islets. The morning cruise departs at 9:30 A.M. and returns at 1:30 P.M. The afternoon cruise stops at an island and also under the massive Niteroi Bridge. The view from this harbor cruise gives you a sense of how the first Portuguese explorers must have been inspired by the beautiful and natural surroundings.

Carnival I put Carnival under things to see. Honestly, I've never made it to Carnival, for the hotel rates double, huge and unruly crowds descend on the city, and the noise never stops. I prefer a little more serene atmosphere, and there is certainly enough to do and see in Rio without the chaos of Carnival. If total hedonism is for you, here are the dates for the next four Carnivals: 1993: February 20; 1994: February 12; 1995: February 25; 1996: February 16.

A good second choice for total craziness is **New Year's Eve,** when Rio goes insane. Imagine every person from San Diego to San Francisco heading for the beach at midnight, standing in the ocean and doing the Samba! I did it in a downpour, and it's one evening I'll never forget. Since this lasts only a day, you miss just one day of sleep and life is back to normal.

Exercising in Rio

Brazil is a body beautiful country — everyone is trying to look better than the other. On the sidewalks, in the parks, and on the beach, everyone is working out. If you enjoy aerobics, weightlifting, and that sweaty gym aura, you won't be disappointed. Almost every street corner has a gym (usually on the upper floor of a larger building), and these are great places to meet Brazilians. Foreigners are very welcome here, since the gyms love foreign currency, and besides, doing aerobics to Samba music is a nice change of pace. Get a recommendation from one of the macho-looking guys at the front desk of your hotel for a good place to go. The third floor of my favorite apartment-hotel (the Aparta Hotel) actually has a gym across from the massage parlor. What a choice in exercise!

Shopping: What to Buy

There are some unusual opportunities in Rio for buying a special gift that is outrageously priced in the States. The best buys are on the street or in the one-of-a-kind boutiques in Ipanema. There are large shopping malls, fairs for the unusual, and even a street lined with antique stores.

Gems   Brazil is known for its amethysts, aquamarines, diamonds, emeralds, topaz, opals and rubies — all of which are found in abundance in Minas Gerais. You pay no duty on gems you buy in Brazil, and you can buy as many as your heart desires. On my last trip I bought a twenty-one pound amethyst rock of deep purple and unusual shape. I considered an amethyst stone so big I could have walked inside it, but I was afraid it would break when I tried to ship it back. One warning: everyone, including your hotel clerk, will be selling stones, so do your shopping carefully and patiently. I recommend buying only what you can carry with you. The cheapest buys are from the back-street shops, but if you don't mind paying a little more, you will find the following stores very reputable: **H. Stern**: handles 65% of all stone business in Brazil and has stores in main hotels and most malls; **Amsterdam Sauer**: honest; the second biggest with the classiest stones. Copacabana Ave.; **Roditi**: reliable; main office Rua Visconde de Piraja, 482, Ipanema.

Remember that stones vary in color, clarity, size, shape, and weight. All of these factors contribute to a determination of a stone's value. If you don't know much about stones, buy the cheapest, for they still make impressive gifts for your friends back home.

Chapter 7

Hippie Fair a Sunday outing with a huge flea market for entertainment, 9:00 A.M. to 6:00 P.M. in the Praca General Osoria, where you'll find hundreds of hand-crafted items displayed in booths. Among my favorites are the paintings of Bahian folk art and the unusual musical instruments. This park is in the center of Ipanema, so you can stroll down to the beach if the sun is too hot. Do watch out for pickpockets.

Street Purchases There is a street fair almost every night in the area of the boardwalk between the Rio Palace Hotel and the Othon Hotel. You can get good buys on leather bags by bargaining, sometimes 20% cheaper than in a store. Sometimes the unusual will show up here, like a fossil I bought my for my sister which was a snake crystallized into a rock. I had to bargain for it for three days to get a reasonable price. You can also buy graphic and pornographic beach towels and tee-shirts.

Specialty items The most famous women's store is called **BUM BUM** on Rua Visconde de Piraja, 437, in Ipanema. Here you'll find that special bathing suit, which of course might be outlawed on the beaches of California. A good place to buy sport clothes is **Cribb Dancing**, either next door to the Othon Hotel or in the huge shopping center, **Rio Sul**, with over 300 stores, movie theaters and restaurants, located in the area of Botafogo, at the end of Princess Isabel, on the other side of the tunnel.

Antiques I'm not a great shopper, but sometimes antique stores can be fun. Due to Brazil's recession, many wealthy people have been forced to pawn or consign their unique lamps, furniture, art, or gold and silver pieces, and so you never know what you'll find. The best street for antiques is Barata Ribeiro, about three blocks back from the beach. This street also offers open-air food markets and massage parlors.

THE NIGHTLIFE OF RIO

There are basically three forms of nightlife in Rio: (1) the tourist spots that specialize in Samba spectaculars and Las Vegas-type productions; (2) intimate cafes, bars, and jazz clubs; and (3) discotheques, varying from the opulent to the "let's get down and boogie." In most hotels you'll find a magazine called "Rio this Month," which gives you up-to-date information on all shows, concerts, and any other activities that are going on that month.

Shows

The most spectacular shows in Rio appear at three establishments: **Scala-Rio**, **Oba-Oba**, and **Plataforma**. **Scala** is the biggest nightclub in Rio, where, beginning at 11:00 P.M., you see all the fancy costumes and topless Mulatas. **Oba-Oba**, in Botafogo, has more of a strip-show atmosphere in a private house. **Plataforma** offers a lot of samba and a history lesson about African culture through colorful displays. Black Orpheus is re-enacted in a carnival events setting. You can make reservations or purchase advance tickets for any of these shows, and all cab drivers know the directions. If you happen to return to the red-light area late at night, at **Bolero**, Ave Atlantica 1910, it's possible to see some of these same girls dancing but this time close enough to touch (and with a big enough wallet, close enough to choose your spot).

If you want something more laid back and don't want to go to Carnival, try **Club do Samba** (65 Estrada da Barra da Tijuca), very informal and fun but a little out of the way. It is run by the best names in Samba and displays the dance in all its forms. The admission is under ten dollars.

Cafes

All along the oceanfront boulevards of Ipanema and Copacabana are the outside cafes that are perfect for meeting women or getting together for a drink or a cheap meal. For as little as the price of a beer, you can stay in one spot all evening. This is a great way to pass the time waiting for the late-night entertainment spots to open. When you want to leave, you have to flag down a waiter to pay your bill.

Chapter 7

Every place has its own personality, the more interesting being: **Barril 1800** (on Ipanema beach, a late-night hang-out for the young and rich); **Jazzmania** (one of the best clubs in Rio, 110 Ave. Vieira Souta, upstairs from Barril 1800); **Garota de Ipanema** (open-air cafe where "The Girl from Ipanema" was written, Rua Vinicius de Moraes, 49).

As for Copacabana, the best way is simply to walk around until you see a crowd that looks interesting. They say the cafes around the Palace Hotel are gay, whereas those in front of the Othon and across the street from the

Spectacular Show

Meridian are heterosexual.
Lucas, Ave. Atlantica 3744,
Copacabana, is popular
among the *fortysomething*
age group.

Bars

Biblo's (Ave. Epitacio
Pessoa, 1484, Lagoa) is
small, friendly, and offers
jazz and a view of the lake
with Christo Redentor
watching every move you
make. Downstairs is
where the action is, and
upstairs has the soft music.

Cozinha internacional e dois conjuntos to-
cando diariamente, tudo isso num ambien-
te sofisticado.

*International cuisine. Two bands
performing for you nightly in a
sophisticated atmosphere.*

Av. Bartolomeu Mitre, 123 – Leblon
Tels.: 239-5789/239-0198

On the other hand, **Let it be**, down the street from the
Aparta Hotel, on 206 Rua Siquiera Campos, Copacabana, is
a noisy, rock-and-roll bar in the image of a Hard Rock Cafe,
right down to the memorabilia. Two other bars in Ipanema
that are worth a stop are **Un Deux Trois** and **People's**, both
high-class meeting spots, the latter being dark and romantic (Ave. Bartolomeu Miter 123 and 370, Leblon.)

Discotheques

I think the discos in Rio are stuffy, expensive, exclusive,
and altogether over-rated. Who attended the discos and
what they wore fill the gossip columns of Rio newspapers.

Caligola (in Ipanema) is probably the most popular with
the jet-set. Here everyone is dressed to impress, so if you
want to see fine Brazilian youth, go to Caligola's. By the
way, the custom in dancing is simply to go and just dance
to the music; it's not necessary to ask someone to dance.
For we American guys, this is strange, but when you ask
someone to dance you will get that "Get lost" look. If a lady
appeals to you — and, believe me, most of them will — just
dance close enough to see if she smiles at you. If she does,
offer her a drink after the music.

Chapter 7

Hippopotamus, the second most popular disco (Rua Barao da Torre), has the slickest dance floor with smoked mirrors reflecting the strobe lights, leopard-skin walls and Amazon flora. (You get the idea; it's not for the underdressed).

On weekends the lines to get into one of these glamour spots can reach the beach, so arrive early or plan to wait a few hours.

Gafieiras

These are dance halls that sprang up in the 1920s as ballrooms for the poor people. Nowadays they are extremely popular with the Cariocas; not only is the entrance fee cheap, but you get to dance to the traditional music. One of the newest and slickest is **Asa Branca**, (Ave. Mem da Sa, 17, in the Lapa region).

Other nightspots

Most hotels have fancy lobby bars, but I find them a little reserved. Just think of it this way: outside are all those beautiful Brazilian women. By the way, all hotels have stringent security; without an escort, many locals are not allowed to enter your hotel.

A SHORT SEXUAL HISTORY

Sometimes I think that men get the wrong idea about the sexual permissiveness of the Brazilian women. They don't chase you down the street and beg for your attention or purposefully dress to make your desire uncontrollable (well, maybe). What makes these women different is their lack of modesty.

Our culture says that women should be generally modest, reserved, and sexually undemonstrative. Brazilian women, however, are not afraid to show off their bodies; in fact, they're proud! They may take a shower with you or show off their carnal knowledge and drive you crazy in three minutes. Encouraging a shy man is their specialty. These women are romantics, unashamed of their bodies, their feelings, or their sexual relations. To fully understand their permissive attitude, I think their history explains much.

After the European discovery of Brazil in the early 1500s, sugar became the main export, and slaves became the status mark of a wealthy plantation baron. From the mid 1550s to the mid 1850s, over 3.5 million blacks were brought to Brazil as slaves. Throughout the seventeenth century, slaves from Africa replaced the Indians as workers, not only because of their superior strength but also because they were more immune to the European diseases. The crop owners ruled colonial Brazil, and even the poor whites that had come over from Portugal even had a few slaves for themselves. The reason for white immigration was obvious: why work and suffer in the Old World where recession and military wars were the norm when you could own other people to do your work for you? Slavery became the selling note of the New World.

The white husband often kept his wife at home while he played the field. Sex between masters and slaves became so prevalent that a new breed developed: the Mulatto. The Mulatto population grew so rapidly because the Church, hoping to increase the sparse population, ignored the blatant infidelities. Even the priests had mistresses and illegitimate children. Add to all of this the fact that there was a shortage of white women, and you begin to understand how Brazil's sexually permissive attitude developed over the years.

Syphillis became rampant and uncontrollable; entire monasteries were wiped out. Many of the free mixed-race women could survive only by selling themselves. As the Bishop of Para stated in one of his letters back home: "...the wretched state of manners in this country puts me in mind of the end that befell the five cities, and makes me think that I am living in the suburbs of Gomorrah, very close indeed, and in the vicinity of Sodam..."

This wretched state of manners doesn't exist today, but the generally permissive attitude toward sex certainly does. A poor Brazilian economy, a body-beautiful consciousness, and a "one day at a time" perception of life make this a man's heaven. This doesn't mean that Brazilian women will obey your every command. Their attitude towards men is unique as they do not prejudge you by your age, color, or nationality. Nowhere in the world can you meet a pretty girl at 1.00 P.M. at an outside cafe and be walking hand in hand half an hour later. The following day she will take you to her favorite club to meet her friends; kissing and fondling all night long with a date you would have given a week's paycheck for at home.

What makes this even more special is that this is not a contrived situation but the way of life. Sleeping together is an afterthought; friendship takes priority. Yes, there are women whom you do pay to play with, but it is also possible to become incredibly close to someone half your age. One of my friends, after an unexpected encounter with a tonga-clad teenager, remembers feeling like a 17 year-old schoolboy, having lost track of time and walking around with a smile from ear to ear. Although he never slept with his teenage sweetie, they still write - that platonic intimacy never died.

WHERE TO FIND THE WOMEN

Finding girls in Rio is no problem; it's only a question of how long you want to wait. If you're in a hurry, then the massage parlors are for you. If you have a little more time, I suggest you read the classified ads in the newspapers (listed under "massage") and start calling until you find Miss Right. Ads that are repetitive and have the same phone number are usually massage parlors willing to send their girls out, for many of the girls live together in the back rooms of the Termas.

Look for ads that are original and phone numbers you haven't seen before. Often these are the numbers of college girls with a little ingenuity, trying to earn extra pin money. With a bit of luck, you might become great friends. These ladies become the perfect guides for the unusual evening establishments, perhaps the trendiest disco, the feastiest new restaurant, or a scenic drive that is not in the guide-book. If you have the evening to do your searching, then you might enjoy the outdoor cafes, in selected locations, or the nightclubs (boites) in the red-light area, or certain discos.

One of my problems is that I'm impatient. So I go to a massage parlor to take care of immediate needs. That makes me less prone to settle for second best during my evening search. Most night women will try to entice you, be

A Brazilian Friend

Chapter 7

patient: the best is yet to come. If you happen to meet a new love late in the evening, you're better off making a lunch appointment if the evening really gets late — romance at 3:00 A.M. is not my idea of a lusty night. Most Brazilian ladies have their own phones and love the idea of an afternoon lunch—a real treat.

If you haven't had your afternoon massage, then you're easy prey for the bar girls, who know every trick (some you wouldn't believe) to weaken your resistance. Eventually you settle for the most aggressive (your libido can take only so much) and you wind up with, well, not the princess you wanted. The more popular massage parlors—in Portuguese, called **termas**—are the following:

Termas L'uomo on Siqueira Campos, 143. Their motto states, "Our specialty is taking good care of you with the most beautiful receptionists and sophisticated ambience."

Termas 65 Rua do Rosario, 65. On the way downtown, the largest and most modern in Rio. They advertise 70 receptionists in a six-story building. On Saturday, the traditional **Feljoadia** (a Brazilian dance show) is included in the price of admission.

Termas Oasis Rua Dezenove de Fevereiro, 123. Billed as the modern executive's paradise with Roman baths, hydro-massage, Sauna, Turkish baths, bar with live music and beautiful ladies at your disposal. The hours are: Monday - Friday 12 a.m. to 12 p.m.; Saturday 12 a.m. to 10 p.m.; Sunday 2 p.m. to 10 p.m.

The massage parlors of Rio are not as sophisticated or elegant as those in Thailand, which you can read about in a later chapter. Their operation, though, is much simpler, as the entrance fee usually covers everything, and the only extras are for drinks and perhaps a tip for special service. Once you enter, you pay from $25 to $50, depending on where the parlor is located (the closer to the beach, the more expensive); how you got there (cab drivers get their cut); and how they perceive you as you enter (can you pass for a Brazilian?) Just keep your mouth shut and point; you'll pay less. Once in, you are given a towel, a receipt, and a locker. After showering, you enter a little bar area where

the girls, in bathing suits, introduce themselves. Don't rush, for you have already paid for whatever you want, and the girls don't get paid unless they get that receipt from you. Once you've picked out your girl, she showers and takes you to a little room where the massage takes place. You normally have up to thirty minutes to have a massage and sex. The girl hopes you'll appreciate her efforts and perhaps give a tip ($5-$10). The tip is often more than she gets from the front office. Afterwards you both shower and maybe you buy her a coke. When you leave, you return the locker key and towel and pay only for the drinks you and your partner have consumed. Now you're ready for the evening and won't be distracted by the first sneaky, sexy girl that approaches you.

Chapter 7

Two last points: Yes, you can call ahead and reserve your favorite girl (for a little extra, you can probably arrange to have her sent to your room), and the girl provides the prophylactic; however, I recommend using an American one that you should have with you. If you don't, then use two of hers, as they are really not up to our standards.

Meeting Girls in Cafes

Cafes are an institution that you must experience to understand. Sitting in a cafe, watching the world go by, and flirting with friends is like Monday night football or the weekend barbecue — it's just what you do to pass time.

In Rio, the cafes also serve as a way of meeting ladies. Obviously the women of Rio know that most men (especially tourists like you) will sooner or later pick a cafe to relax in; this is the perfect time for an amateur to try her luck. What makes this so much fun is that you never know whom you are talking to: it might be a lonely housewife, or a college girl or even one in high school, or just someone curious, looking for a friend or dance partner for the evening. Or it might be a professional prostitute, or even a trans-sexual. You have to figure out which is which. The hustlers are obvious, winking and staring at you; sometimes they just come over to your table and introduce themselves. The amateurs usually aren't very aggressive because they are somewhat embarrassed about asking for money.

If you see a lady you like, even if she's not looking your way, it's perfectly normal to walk over and ask to join her or her group for a drink. If she's an amateur, she'll be happy you made the first move. Cafe society moves very slowly; talking, drinking, feeling out the situation is quite normal for both parties.

The later in the evening, the greater the choices; the best cafes are full until 11:00 P.M. The top choices for ladies of easy persuasion are the cafes in front of the large hotels —Othon, Rio Palace — and across the street from the Meridian. The best cafes are from the Copacabana Palace to the Meridian. The back streets here are the red-light zone with a few "boites" on Ave. Atlantica. This cafe flirting is possibly the best way to meet a lady, as you don't have to pay a bar fine (in boites there is a fee for taking a lady out of the bar and a minimum-number-of-drinks fee, $20+).

A word to the wise: negotiate a price *before* arriving at your room; you'll save money and avoid misunderstanding and frustration. Also, most girls will ask you, even if their home is across the street, for taxi money. This is their way of asking for a tip for good service. If it wasn't what you expected or a major disappointment, don't tip.

The girls you meet in cafes can often become friends and you may wind up spending the next day on the beach with them. You may even become friendly with their friends. Careful, now! Don't take more than one girl at a time to your room! It's tempting; the old menage à trois, quatre, cinq, but it's impossible to watch them all when you're occupied, and guaranteed, the next morning a camera, radio, or other valuable will be gone. Let me suggest that you go to one of the hotels that rent rooms by the hour, where the worst that could happen is that they take a towel.

If you go for more than one, it isn't hard. Brazilian women are not bashful. Be sure that the price you settle on is for both. I once fell into the trap of getting too anxious and later found out the negotiation was per person, a major setback for my pocketbook.

Cafe society is like a fine wine. You must sip it slowly, whirl it around in your mouth, think about it, and once you understand it, drink the bottle. At first, this new pastime seems wasteful, but once you get the feel, it becomes a Brazilian addiction.

Meeting Girls in the Boites

The boites are basically small nightclubs with a wide range of activities: from simple strip-tease to scantilly clad disco-samba dancers; and from quiet drinking bars to pick-up bars, some with live sex shows. The names border on the ridiculous: *Pussy Cat Bar, Las Vegas, Erotika, Munich, Night and Day.*

Chapter 7

Actually they can be quite fun. Most are located in Copacabana's red-light district, which is bordered by Ave. Atlantica, Ave. Princess Isabel, and Ave Copacabana. My downtown favorite is **Assyrius**, very large and elegant, where you'll find roving bar girls and many couples watching the acts. The best system is to walk in and ask what time the show is. The door man will let you in to look around without pressuring you to sit down and have a drink.

I consider **Barbarela**, Ave. Princess Isabel 263 to be one of the five best bars in the world. This place really gets packed after 11:00 P.M. You'll need to pay an entrance fee, drinks for you and your lady, a bar fee for her to leave with you, and of course her pin money—an easy $150 for the evening, but every man, once in his lifetime, should have at least the opportunity to try and say no to these girls. The price includes fashion shows at 1:00 A.M. and 3:00 A.M. that allow you to see everyone together. This is the kind of place where if there is someone you fancy but she doesn't notice you (after all, it's crowded and noisy), simply tip the waiter and ask him to bring her to you. Most of these women are students, secretaries, housewives, and models who aren't doing too well, all trying to earn a little extra to supplement their normal jobs.

A more mellow second choice is **Scherezade**, Ave. N. S. Copacabana 187-A, on the corner of Ronald Carvalho across from the park. This is a small bar, intimate and unusually quiet for Rio, basically serving a Japanese clientele, but they are more than happy to serve you drinks. The girls will leave you alone, unless you ask for company.

A reminder - once you buy a girl a drink, you are hers; no other girl will approach you. So make sure she is the one you would like to talk to. If you want to drink alone, just say so. Here again, the emphasis is on strikingly beautiful women. In both of these bars the women could easily pass for your wife, so getting them into a five-star hotel is possible. Remember to agree on a price before you leave the bar. A good tactic is to get your princess's phone number (usually it's very late by the time you get this far) and make arrangements for lunch with high promises. The advantage here is you don't have to pay the bar fee, and there is no competition because you're one-on-one. During lunch she'll be much more reasonable, and you two will have time to get to know each other. Also, getting a girl to your room in mid-afternoon is usually no problem, as security assumes she's your wife or you're just going to the pool. Always have lunch by the pool, as you're half-way to your room, and security takes it for granted that she's checked in with you. By the way, let's say it's been rainy for a few days and your lady is supposed to meet you for lunch. If the sun comes out, she won't show up or she will be at least two hours late. Once you do get her to your room, amazingly her panties will be her tonga bathing-suit. This way she gets the best part of both worlds — sun and a little pin money.

Another option is **HELP Discotheque** (Ave. Atlantica 3432), next to the Othon Hotel in the middle of Copacabana. Outside is one of the best cafes. At 11 p.m. everyone starts lining up for the disco. This dance hall is perhaps the largest in South America. Around midnight a few hundred amateurs will probably be checking you out. Since the entrance fee is nominal (a few dollars), this is the hang-out for the young and restless women who would rather be dancing than sitting as they look for eligible (i.e. financially supportive) men. Even if you aren't in the mood, this is a great place just to dance and have a good time. Remember, you need not ask a lady to dance; just go on to the dance floor. As Bo says, *just do it!*

Other than these places, the other boites go downhill as does the price of the ladies. Some of the bars are tacky and disgusting, others are lustfully exotic. There are always bar-girls trying to capture your attention, but after **Barbarela** and **Scherezade**, you'll be hard to please. Remember, you get what you pay for in the bars.

There are many other clubs, bars, cafes and discos all through Rio, and they all function in about the same way. If you see a beautiful lady on the street, in a shopping mall, or even in the bank, don't be afraid to start a conversation. The worst she can do is ignore you, but more than likely she will be as curious about you as you are about her.

Chapter 7

Where to Take Your Girl

This seems like a stupid subject, but actually it's very important. Many five-star hotels will not accept outside girls (there have been problems, such as theft, excessive noise, usage of drugs). This creates a problem if you want to stay in a nice place yet entertain guests. First, ask your friendly bellboy the hotel policy, for it can be embarrassing to ask the front-desk manager when there's a crowd around. Bellboys know all the tricks and schemes for these operations and might even help you in a desperate situation (he could bring her to your room as a friend). Obviously a tip is in order for his needed help.

Another possibility, which all the girls know, is that there are hotels on the back streets of Copacabana that rent rooms by the hour. These rooms are clean and comfortable and run about $20/hr. This is the perfect solution for those lusty women or for the ones whose character you haven't yet determined. I've had friends of insatiable lust who rent a cheap room in addition to their ocean-front suite. It's possible to get a room in a two-star hotel for about $30/ night and have the best of both worlds.

Of course, the best alternative is the Apart Hotel, as I've stated previously. Don't go to the girl's residence unless you've known her for awhile. Once a friend of mine left a girl's room at around 3:00 A.M. He had followed her home with the promise of a wild orgy, but after a quickie, which cost him his last hundred dollars, he left with no idea of where he was, and no money for a taxi, and no taxis running anyway, and three unknown men following him; lucky for him an off-duty taxi stopped when he waved it down. Don't let lust confuse your good sense.

My favorite solution is the afternoon nap. Security in most deluxe hotels is relaxed during the day and, as I've said, meeting new friends for lunch by the pool is common. After lunch, its usually an easy walk to your room to change bathing attire (in case you are questioned, this is the perfect answer). I like this procedure because it gives you some time to get to know the lady you met at 2:00 in the morning on the previous night. Seeing her in daylight and sober might make you change your mind about romantic involvement. It's easy to say no - just say, "the management said it was impossible".

Do not:

- *Pick up a girl at night hitch-hiking - she is a guy!*

- *Be a show off - you'll only be charged more and become a target for thieves.*

- *Leave a new friend unattended in your room. Shower together when you are finished and your watch will remain by your bed.*

OTHER DESTINATIONS WITHIN BRAZIL

You need to spend at least a week in Rio to get to know it. But, Brazil is almost the size of the United States. There is so much more to see in this country that you could tour it for a month.

If you can afford the time and want to travel around, I suggest you purchase an air-pass before leaving the U.S., from Varig, Transbrazil, or VASP (one air-pass per airline and not interchangeable). With a Brazil Air-pass ticket you can visit any five cities in Brazil within a 24 day period, currently for $440. This is a good price; think about the cost of a flight from L.A. to New York to Miami to Seattle to New Orleans and back to L. A. with no restrictions! It is a bargain. Remember you must purchase your air-pass voucher in the United States before you depart.

Chapter 7

Buzios

This is my only place on my list where you won't need the air-pass. In the district of Cabo Frio, about three hours from Rio, this is the resort that Brigitte Bardot made famous about thirty years ago. The city and beach of Cabo Frio is fun, as it's a Brazilian holiday town that is packed in high season and crazy. Buzios is for the upscale who want to get away from the crowds, the noise, and the pollution of Rio, and just relax. The roads are unpaved, but there are 27 sandy coves, with crystal clear water, and 17 beaches for your enjoyment.

The small town has a Santa Fe feel, with artists, musicians, small boutiques, trendy restaurants, and nightclubs. Once a small fishing village, Buzios has neither the large hotels (you stay in small inns called *pousadas*), nor the glitzy nightlife yet. Get there before it does. Your local travel agent can do all the hotel and transportation booking, but compare prices.

Salvador

If you have time to see only one other city in Brazil, go to Salvador. Called the true soul of Brazil, this city of nearly two million is the cradle of Macumba, and it features unbelievable local cuisine and exotic festivities. Many people consider Salvador's carnival superior to Rio's.

African influences are everywhere since this was the main slave port in colonial times. Most of the plantation barons' wealth was used to build and decorate the colossal public buildings, the ornate squares, and the intriguing African-Catholic churches that are everywhere. The city, only a few hours from Rio by jet, sits on the southern tip of a V-shaped peninsula; most of the people live on the coast. A steep hill divides central Salvador into two parts: the upper, Ciadade Alta (where it's a continuous party), and the lower, Ciadade Baixa. An elevator connects the two parts, with the bottom being the commercial and financial center (including a colorful market) while upstairs is where the people live. At night the bottom is desolate while the suburb is a spontaneous party with Candomble (African religious services) and street dancing.

As for eating, Dende, an African palm oil is used to cook delicious spicy regional dishes. A suburb called **Barra**, with its outdoor bars and discos, is the place for the tourist at night. The beach continues for miles, and of course the best, **Itapoa**, is the one farthest from town.

Close to the international airport, called Dois de Julho, is one of the best hotels in Brazil, **Quatro Rodas**, which you'll also find in Sao Luis and Olinda. Closer to town are the **Othon** and **Meridian** hotels, each in a small cove with its own beach. This area, called Ondina, is close enough to walk to Barra yet interesting enough to make you want to stay put. I suggest a city tour to gain some perspective on the confusing one-way streets, the hills, and the crazy drivers. A fun excursion is a ferry to the island **Itaparica**, where there is a Club Med, but this is very crowded on weekends.

Sometimes Salvador is called Bahia, but actually you're in the state of Bahia, and Salvador is its capital. The weather is always hot and humid, which makes the sultry Capoeeira dance (an African self-defense ritual blended with a disco fever) exciting to watch. Second only to Rio in visual beauty, coupled with original music, fascinating buildings, unbelievable food, hordes of partying women, and some pristine beaches, Salvador is an adventure worth taking!

Brasilia

A monument of how to waste money, some 600 miles northwest of Rio, Brasilia was built from scratch in 1960, designed like an airplane with the wings as the satellite living areas. The new capital of Brazil is, as far as I can see, a total failure. Everything is planned, down to the bench in the park.

This city is a tomb of unrealistic expenses; to this day Brasilia is one of the major causes of Brazil's tremendous foreign debt. Most Brazilian cities have unique personalities, and this city is what we would call a geek—no color or identity. The famous architect, Oscar Niemeyer, designed all the major buildings; if you like the look of the U.N. (which he also designed), you'll like this city too.

Here there is a sector for everything—hotels, leisure, camping, education and government. One advantage is its compactness, which makes it easier to see in one day and then leave. The social and economic costs of building and supplying Brasilia (it's in the middle of nowhere) have made the poor even poorer and the government even more separated from its people. In my opinion this city is so unrealistic (and no fun compared to other cities in Brazil) that only a person who would enjoy living in a concrete airplane could enjoy this capital. I put it in this section only because people always ask what I thought of Brasilia? Now I can answer: it's not worth the stop on your air-pass.

São Luis

This is a beautiful, friendly city of colonial charm, rich in folklore, with great beaches and unique hotels. Picture New Orleans in the 1800s: fresh fish and fruit markets, tile roofs, cobblestone streets and wrought-iron balconies —this is São Luis today.

Unfortunately, São Luis is one of the poorest cities in all of Brazil. Its one-way streets are grimy with holes everywhere, electricity doesn't work most of the time, the city center is decaying, the people are shabbily dressed, and you wonder what the strange aromas are.

So what's good about it? Well, first there are no tourists. In the kinky brothels you might be the only American they've seen. In June their carnival, *Bumba meu Boi*, is truly unique, for its colors, smells, costumes, and dance are performed only here. Most of the city's charm lies in its history. Its colonial architecture is unrivaled in Brazil. The only city in Brazil to be settled by the French, which is why it's similar to New Orleans, and briefly occupied by the Dutch, it became an important sugar- and cotton-exporting center for the Portuguese in 1615.

Today it's a relic of history with two great hotels. **Quatro Rodas**, on Praia do Calhau, is a full-fledged resort with pool, convention facilities, tennis courts, and lovely gardens. What makes it also special is its beach. When the tide goes out on Praia do Calhau, you think you could walk to Africa; when it comes back in, the beach disappears; this is an amazing sight that happens every day.

If, however, you want to be in the middle of the action, rather than fifteen minutes away at Quatro Rodas, then the **Villa Rica Hotel** is for you. Downtown, across from the park and the lusty cafes connected by hilly cobblestone streets, this is a gorgeous hotel with a huge circular pool and fine restaurants. Make sure to ask for a room overlooking the bay. From here all the treasures of São Luis are within walking distance. Again, Varig Airlines can make all the reservations for you at good discounts.

The Amazon Cities

This river with its tributaries is one of the great natural wonders of the world. Amazonia covers two million square miles and from its origin high in the Andes runs more than 4,000 miles until it empties into the Atlantic Ocean. The second-longest river in the world (the Nile is the first), the Amazon contains inlets, islands, beaches, all types of animal and fish life, tropical rain forests, and two of the more interesting cities in the world.

Manaus At the moment, this is a city of faded glory. At one time it was king of the rubber trade. Its buildings were brought over piecemeal from London and Paris, giving it a real European flair. Today it's a dirty and run-down city, but the harbor is still vibrant, colorful, and delightfully seedy. Be sure to behold the "Meeting of the Waters" close to Manaus; here the black water of the Rio Negro and the brown water of the Rio Solimoes meet in a unique whirlpool that takes four miles before it becomes one Amazon River.

There is an international airport that has connections via Varig Airlines and VASP with Miami and Los Angeles. A wonderful hotel, the **Tropical Manaus,** with its own Amazon zoo, a parkland filled with vegetation, and river guides for the Amazon lies a short distance from the airport, but a distance from the city. Reservations can be made through Varig Airlines.

Belem Gateway to the Amazon, 90 miles from the open sea, Belem was the first European settlement, founded in 1616, on the Amazon, and was designed to handle all the shipping and trade going up the river. It is filled with colonial architecture, and its main avenue (President Vargas) is full of mango trees. The Avenue leads you to the 300-year-old Ver-o-peso market. An old-fashioned opera house (Teatro da Paz) with Victorian marble statues, and the charming Parca da Republic, a local park surrounded by mango trees and the main gathering place of the city, are also located on the street. Here you'll find the main restaurants and bars for a lusty night-life. The **Hilton** is the best hotel, and close to you is a fascinating zoo and a real jungle park of virgin forest.

The port area, which is either long walk or short cab ride away, looks as if time has frozen the last 300 hundred years. Ships take on cargo (herbs, fruits, fish, alligator teeth, and dried roots) for that up-river run. The mixture of exotic aromas is impossible to forget. By the way, it rains almost every day, but it's refreshing and predictable.

Other Cities .

During my last trip to Brazil, I decided to use an airpass to see the beach cities along the north coast. In addition to Sao Luis, I visited **Recife**, an upcoming Rio-type city with a beach called Boa Viagen that is as fun as Copacabana; **Fortaleza**, known for its lace works; **Natal,** the new Brazilian tourist center with miles of sand dunes and the newest hotels in Brazil; **Maceio**, with crystal clear water and protecting reefs; and **Joao Pessoa**, with the most unusual hotel in all of Brazil. I can't overemphasize how enjoyable and adventurous I found each of these, and so let me describe a few of my favorite north coast beach cities in detail.

Fortaleza The most lusty of the northern cities. An evening beer on the promenade provides the perfect vantage point to find your evening companion - they just keep strolling by and smiling. In front of the "Othon" hotel is best - (085-224-7777). The only problem is that the city lacks luster and the main beach is poor. Many visitors prefer the "Praio do Futuro" beach for accommodations with a visit to Forteleza for the night-life, a five dollar cab ride.

Natal The best Friday - Saturday night action city. The main street, Avenida 25 Decembre, becomes a sort of Hollywood Boulevard on weekend nights. This is where the Brazilians come to vacation, especially the good girls who want to temporarily become bad girls. A real bonus are the magnificent beaches: Arista, for high waves and closeness to town; Pirangi beach, where you can see the biggest cashew tree in the world; Genipabu beach, famous for its sand dunes and lakes; and my favorite **Ponta Negra,** situated about seven miles south from town, off the freeway called Via Costeria. Close to the airport are endless beaches, centered around a bohemian village, separate from Natal, which is full of all night cafes, bars, and wild dance parties. Sometimes these spontaneous orgies flow into the street and end in the water. I stayed at "LAINAS PLACE" which is an all-suite hotel with fabulous views, a quaint pool, and free breakfast that lasts all day. The owner speaks English (an ex-American soccer coach) and will even pick you up at the airport! (084) 236-3349.

Joao Pessoa Located between Natal and Recife, this city has its claim to fame with a point of land called the "Gravel Point," which is the easternmost landfall in the Western Hemisphere. The city itself is boring, but there are some fascinating coves called *enseadas* that form a 15-mile beach front a few miles east of the city center. The best known area is called Tambau where you'll find one of my favorite hotels, **Hotel Tambau.** This ocean front horseshoe-shaped hotel has walls that buttress the sea and comes complete with two pools (one solely for water polo), game rooms, verandas, tennis and a two-level courtyard. I always

Chapter 7

A northern beauty

get lost in this circular maze but the architecture is amazing. Owned by Varig Airlines, they can make your hotel reservation. (083-226-3660).

Olinda The Santa Fe of Brazil, situated on a hill overlooking **Recife** and the Atlantic ocean. The village has been declared a national monument, which means the pink stucco and fancy wood trim of the houses cannot be changed. Here you'll find musicians, artists, local craftsmen, antique shops, funky restaurants, and all sorts of *"Pousadas"* — old time homes that rent out rooms. During your evening stroll you'll encounter countless kids offering to be your guide. Hire one, for not only does he disperse the young gatherers but he will certainly have a sister!

The negative aspect of this relatively unknown colonial gem is that it is a good forty-five minutes to an hour from the Recife airport. The bonus is that it has one of the best hotels in all of the North Coast, **Quatro Rodas Olinda**. Located on the ocean with an usually great pool, tennis courts, and a very active beach front; I was enticed to a boat cruise with a guarantee of a beautiful companion. The deluxe rooms are like mini-suites and the hotel manager is an avid tennis player. In fact, in Brazil it's easy to find tennis courts but quality players are difficult. (081-431-2955).

GETTING HOME

Again, never ask a taxi driver to hurry to the airport if you're returning from Rio. You are giving him an invitation to prove he is the world's greatest race car driver. Arrive early because there are lots of security check points and long lines.

Your Brazilian money is worthless in the States, so give any left-over to the janitor (he'll always remember you). Hopefully you've reconfirmed your return flight. By the way, never allow your girl friend to send you off; for some reason it always ends up with your giving her your last $20 bill and a promise (which is hard to keep and no one likes to lie) to write and come back soon. And yes, she will want you to promise to send for her soon because she can't live without you.

But you will return, because it's impossible to see much of Brazil in one or two trips. Once hooked, you'll be continually returning. After spending last summer in Europe, I only regret that I didn't spend it in Brazil. As they say, "so little time and so much to see," or, in the case Brazil, it should say "so many women and so little time!"

Thailand: Fun in Bangkok

Thailand evokes an intense love-hate reaction in many people. Bangkok, the capital, has been called the "city of angels," but like its sister city Los Angeles, it might be called hell: between the unbelievable traffic, smog and foul air, noise pollution, and a national inability to plan long-term, you might wonder how anyone could live there. Sometimes a cab ride to the river, just a few miles, can take hours, and the noise of the Tuk-Tuks — the two-stroke motorbikes with a cargo bin for two — can drive you crazy. Having to wear long pants in 90% humidity makes simple tasks monumental. This city of sin, origin of the song "A Night in Bangkok," is also quite conservative. Provocative dress is frowned upon, women will never look you in the eye, and you could stroll around for days without meeting a lovely until you get to the bar area. So why go?

First, Thailand is historically special. It is the only southeast Asian country that was never a European colony, and one of the few to emerge from World War II unscathed, because the Thai government gave in immediately to Japan to avoid bloodshed. The unique culture of Thailand has developed slowly over the last 700 years, and its Buddhist religion, practiced by 90% of the population, endorses the Thai's strong identity. Thailand, which means *Land of the Free,* was first made famous to Westerners by the story "Anna and the King of Siam" and later by the famous R & R (rest & relaxation) centers for our Vietnam soldiers. The people are polite, deeply gracious, kind, and understanding to the "Farang" (foreigner) and truly convey the image of the "land of smiles." Called *Sanuk,* this is one of the first things you notice about Thailand - a big smile. Even when it's your mistake in the restaurant or your misunderstanding in a bar, you'll get that big, beautiful, shy smile.

In Thailand, religion is the way of life and rural Thais spend a quarter of their income on religious activities. The Thai form of Buddhism puts special emphasis on doing good deeds and performing special tasks. An example might be giving food to the monks, helping build a wat (temple) or doing special tasks, hoping for a better spot in the next life. In Buddhism, making merit erases negative Karma as one moves toward perfect knowledge — *Nirvana.* Even freeing a captured bird or tortoise is worth merit. Most men are supposed to be monks for three months. If you get up early in the morning you'll see them walking the streets, accepting small gifts of food from their followers.

To truly understand the Thai mentality, one must shift thinking gears. On one hand, they smoke heavily, and they don't wear motorcycle helmets. On the other hand, why worry about dying when your afterlife may be better? If you lead a good religious life, respect your elders, support younger ones, surely you will go to a better life. A hotel manager in Phuket explained to me that Thais don't believe in preventive maintenance, the thought being, why waste time fixing something that will eventually break anyway?

Thailand is like a beautiful, naive child quickly growing up in the modern world. Its economy today is one of the fastest growing in all of Asia, with four consecutive years of growth, due in part to cheap labor that attracts Japanese investments. This year, even with the Gulf war, rising oil prices, a slump in tourism, and a coup, Thailand is still one of the economic leaders in the world at 8 percent annual growth. So, while the traffic moves slowly, apparently the Buddhist religion has nothing against hard work and making money.

The first time you travel to Bangkok, you may end up like your first trip anywhere: a disaster. But over the years the city will grow on you with its exotic temples, smells of roses, spicy foods, and who-knows-what from the open-air markets. There is adventure around every corner, and, of course, some of the most beautiful women in the world.

Although Thailand is just a little bigger than California, (a difference of only 20,000 square miles), there is so much to see: beautiful beaches to the south, remote islands, tropical jungles, mountain valleys, ancient sites, and true bargain shopping. One can go trekking in the Golden Triangle, swim in crystal clear water of Phuket, or visit ancient sites in the northern mountain cities of Chiang Mai and Chiang Rai. You can visit sex-oriented beach resorts of Pattaya — the most degenerate resort on the face of this earth — or merely join the locals in Hua Hin where the elite Thais vacation, a three-hour drive from Bangkok. You can see the forests, waterfalls, caves and jungle in Kanchanaburi province, where the bridge over the River Kwai was built. You can take a river boat up to Ayutthaya — the magnificent ruins of ancient Thailand and the former capital. New beach resorts like Koh Sumui (with its new airport) in the Gulf and Krabi or Phuket in the Andaman Sea make for unparalleled beach jaunts.

I've taken three trips to Thailand, and I'm just beginning to understand the beauty of the country. At first glance, it may seem like an ugly duckling, but once you get a feel for the natural surroundings, experience the peaceful people, and accept Bangkok for what it is, you'll want to come back again and again. The manner in which the Thai people respect life makes you realize that maybe there is still something for you to learn.

Just recently, Prime Minister Chatichai Choonhaven's government was overthrown in a bloodless coup. He alienated the people and the military, it is alleged, by corruption, bribes, and payoffs in Bangkok's tremendous expansion. Although this is the end of three years of supposed democ-

Chapter 8

racy, it is now hoped that the massive pollution, noise, and unchecked construction will end and reason will be restored. This is the seventeenth coup in the last sixty years, yet the promotion of tourism is still paramount to the new government. In fact, with all the new hotels, resorts, and expanded airline services, now is the perfect time to visit.

Remember, be it political or environmental uncertainties, staying in Bangkok proper is not necessary to the enjoyment of Thailand. Besides, the airport is thirty miles from the city center and surrounded by two great hotels (the Airport Hotel, adjacent by a skywalk, and the Rama Gardens, a few miles away). There is also a fabulous new international airport in Phuket. If you must arrive at the Bangkok International, hire a cab ($50 - $75 but bargain hard) and head straight to Pattaya. Here the hotels are half the price of Bangkok, and you can make up the expensive cab ride in two nights. You can relax on the beach away from noise and pollution, and be entertained by more nocturnal activities than time allows.

CLIMATE

Thailand, known until 1949 as Siam, is about half a million square miles, and borders Burma (Myanmar), Laos, Kampuchea (formerly Cambodia), and to the south Malaysia. With a population of 55 million (10% of whom live in Bangkok), Thailand is still an agrarian society where climate is very important. The country is divided into four parts: the fertile central plain, the northern mountains, the diverse south, and the semi-arid northeast. I recommend spending most of your time in the south and in Bangkok. The corresponding weather is:

Bangkok October through February is the cool season (and the high tourist season too), after which it gets hot and sticky in March through June. Then June through September are very wet, and you practically need a canoe. So, remember the three main seasons roughly as February to May (hot), June to October (rainy), and November through

January (cool). When I say cool, it never goes below 75 degrees Fahrenheit, and most evenings you don't need a sweater.

Phuket and the South Here it's always hot and humid, but like Bangkok, from May to October, watch out for monsoon season; it's possible that strong rain and wind will ruin your beach holiday. It's best to visit the beaches after the rains when the bug population has died down. The perfect time is March and April, for the European tourists are starting to leave and the hotel rates are more reasonable (although high season is November through February — after Chinese New Year, when hordes of vacationers descend). A second choice would be October, as then the rains are intermittent and even refreshing while hotel rates are rock bottom.

Northern Mountains and Chiang Mai This is the major northern mountain city where it does get cool (possibly below 65) in the winter months. Although I won't say much about this city, it is noted for having the prettiest girls in Thailand. Chiang Mai is also the perfect starting point for a hike into the lush mountains and tropical forests near the Golden Triangle.

GETTING THERE

First the good news: there are endless choices of airlines to Thailand, and the new Asian market has been completely deregulated. You can choose from the U.S. carriers United, Delta, and Northwest, or you can try an exotic airline like Singapore, Korean, Cathay Pacific (an excellent Hong Kong carrier that just started non-stop flights from LAX to Hong Kong), China Air, Philippine Air, JAL, ANA (a new Japanese carrier), Malaysia Air, and even Thai Airways. China Airlines (800-227-5118) recently began flying the new Boeing 747-400's daily non-stop, LAX to Taipei, with a quick connection to Bangkok. I recommend that you definitely shop around and compare ticket prices between travel agents, consolidators, and airline promotions.

Chapter 8

Now the bad news: it's a very long flight. Even the new Boeing 747-400's can't make it to Bangkok from the west coast without a stop. Flying time can vary from 16 to 20 hours, depending on the routing. If you get stuck on the ground, as you always do at Tokyo's Narita Airport, the trip can take 25 hours. Once, due to new security measures, my flight missed its connection in Seoul, and it took 35 hours to get home. This is the last time I'll mention Korean Airlines. I'm a firm believer in the old saying, if you don't have anything good to say, don't talk.

Obviously it's also worth it to see more than one Asian city if you have the time. All airlines will allow free stops at their hubs if you tell them in advance. You might consider stopping at Tokyo, Seoul, Hong Kong, Taipei, Manila, or Singapore. Thai Airways usually offers purchasers outside Thailand a multi-destination ticket. Currently, for $239 you can fly on any four sectors of Thai's domestic network. Extra domestic destinations are $50; check Thai Airways for their latest promotion. (800-426-5204).

Also ask what kind of plane you will be flying on and what its seating pattern is like. For example, Delta seats ten across in their new MD 11, which means your seat is 18.5 inches wide and has a pitch of 31 inches. Their first two Asian bound planes were leased but their new one will have 9-across seating and a pitch of 33 inches. Thai Airways flies the same plane, but they've reduced the number of seats across, so that each seat is 19.5 inches wide and has a pitch of 34 inches. The extra room can be very important on a long, long flight. Seating patterns may be 2-5-2 (as on the MD 11 or DC 10) or 3-4-3 (as on most 747's). Call your airline and discuss seat selections. Avoid getting stuck in the middle. Remember Murphy's Law: if there are two sick teenagers or crying babies on the plane, they'll be on either side of you.

If you don't mind spending a few extra hundred dollars (it seems the better of the more popular airlines don't discount to consolidators) I'd suggest an Asian airline. This is not American bashing but Asian carriers do provide a better product. Singapore (800-742-3333), Cathay Pacific (800-233-2742), and Thai (800-426-5204) provide excellent service and are rated in the top ten in the world. Thai Airlines just started service in new McDonnell Douglas MD 11's from Los Angeles, and has some good promotional rates. One of the highest honors an Asian girl can receive is to be picked to fly her country's national carrier, as it's a great way to see the world and meet new people.

You might also want to consider one of the Frequent Flyer Clubs so many airlines offer. Northwest (800-447-4747) is currently offering a free domestic ticket with a round-trip to Asia. United (800-241-6522) has the most flights to Asia, and when you purchase a round-trip, they allow you a free feeder flight to the departing hub, for example, Santa Barbara to San Francisco. Now is the perfect time to check for upgrade coupons to business class. Since a business class ticket is usually three times the price of economy and the flight will indeed be long, it is certainly worth it to give up your miles for an upgrade.

Be careful though with schedules, as the flight you may get can actually have a better alternate route. An example is United flight #845, which flies from San Francisco to Taipei to Bangkok in a brand new 747-400 in less than 17 hours even with the short stop in Taiwan. But Flight #837 leaves San Francisco an hour or so later, stops in Tokyo for three hours before arriving in Bangkok at 12:30 a.m. in an older 747-100.

The cheapest flights are usually on Korean Airlines, which I don't recommend, and on China Air. Make sure to ask the price of one of the preferred flights; sometimes there are specials or the difference between regular and preferred is nominal. Or check into tickets sold by the consolidators. Some of the more reliable consolidators are:

McSon Travel. Chicago. 800-622-1421.

Euro Asia Express. San Francisco. 800-782-9624 or 800-878-8538.

OC Tours. San Francisco. 800-878-8718 (outside California, call 800-222-5292).

International Travel. Los Angeles. 213-837-1101.

Jetair. 800-4-JETAIR. Discounts on business class.

Chapter 8

*In Thailand, you can find tour operators like **Chawla Travel** on Patpong 2 (233-4328) or **Diethelm Travel** on 140 Wireless (255-9150) who will take care of your tickets, reconfirmations, hotel vouchers, reservations, sightseeing, and travel planning.*

A Note about the Bangkok Airport

The airport, **Don Muang**, has just had a major renovation and expansion. International flights are in one building, domestic flights are in another, and long walks are the norm. Supposedly there is a shuttle service, but it was never there when I needed it. A word of warning: apparently all international flights arrive at the same time, and passing through immigration can take up to an hour. From the airport to downtown Bangkok is about 25 minutes if there is no traffic, which is only at eleven o'clock at night, so allow a minimum of an hour each way. A nice convenience is a bag storage facility: for a few dollars a day the airport stores your bag while you're out touring the country.

Outside the terminals are the taxis. They will take you to Bangkok or all the way to Pattaya if you want. Inside the terminals are schedules and booths for the buses, but don't bother as they take forever. Take a taxi. Once in Bangkok, the best way to get around is to walk it, smell it, listen to it, observe it, one section at a time. Walking is very safe here.

Flying into Phuket

If the thought of dealing with the chaos of Bangkok turns you off and all you want are crystal waters, natural wonders, room service, and beautiful women, consider Phuket, perhaps the premier beach resort in the world. Phuket just opened its new international airport, an hour's flight from Bangkok. Thai Airways has nine flights daily, and there are now 36 direct international flights per week from Singapore, Penang (the Malaysian beach resort which in no way compares to Phuket), Hong Kong, Taipei, and

Kuala Lumpur (the Malaysian capital, often abreviated KL). Dragon Air makes the connection from Hong Kong, and Trade Winds Air (reservations through Singapore Airline) makes it from Singapore. Thai Air and Malaysian Air fly through Kuala Lumpur to Phuket on alternate days. Phuket airport, small, charming and hassle free, is a great way to bypass crazy Bangkok, although I still recommend that everyone see and experience Bangkok at least once.

The most direct flight to Phuket from Los Angeles is China Airlines (800-227-5118). Their afternoon flight arrives in Taipei early the following evening, because of the time change. They put you in a hotel for the night (no visa is needed) and then fly you to Phuket at 10:30 the next morning. Hotel accommodations are included in your airline ticket.

BASIC INFORMATION ABOUT BANGKOK

First, it worthwhile knowing that Bangkok has two excellent English papers, The Post and The Nation. If you want to get the low-down on Thai night-life, the "Trink" - page in the Saturday Bangkok Post gives you the latest on all the bars, clubs, and attractions. Also the magazine, Where, in your hotel room or at the front desk, gives you the latest happenings and the best restaurants.

Money

The unit of currency, called the *baht*, has been very stable over the last ten years and is pegged at 25 to the dollar (no black market). American money can be changed easily at banks, stores, and hotels. If you run out of money (as I have twice with all the great buys), the American Express office will cash your personal check. Also, most credit cards are recognized, and traveler's checks are welcome. A new wrinkle is the non-automated ATM's. Local exchange houses (almost on every corner) will let you take a direct draw on your Visa or Master card: in other words, a human ATM.

Chapter 8

Passport/Visa

You do need a passport to enter the country, but no visa is necessary unless you're staying more than 15 days. On my last trip I overstayed this period (I was having such a good time that I just couldn't leave) and found out at the airport that a daily nominal fee must be paid for stays over the 15 days. This was a better solution than wasting time trying to get a visa for a few days.

If you can't stand to leave, you can extend your stay by getting an extension at the Immigration Division in Soi Suan Phlua (286-7003 or 386-4230). If you stay only a few extra days and don't want to bother with long lines, the Immigration Department at the airport will charge you $4/day for stays over two weeks. It's advisable not to try to extend your stay for more than a week, in which case you should get a visa.

Food

Food is a real treat, as Thai cuisine is hot and spicy, with loads of shellfish, fruits and vegetables, a cross between Indian, Chinese, Portuguese, French and Indonesian. Of course, you can always ask for milder versions. Don't forget the local street fairs, where a quick taste at the noodle shop or pavement food-stall is a treat. My favorite is Pad Thai—fried noodles, vegies, onions, and spicy peanuts. Most food is already cut into small pieces; thus a knife is unnecessary. Also, salt is rarely used, so add a little Nam-Pla (caramel-colored fish sauce) and smile.

Water

It is recommended not to drink the water, not because it's dirty but because the Asian spices and bacteria can trouble a Westerner's stomach (just as Mexicans often get sick on our water when they come to the United States).

Crime

Security is normally not a problem, but in certain areas where drugs are sold or large crowds congregate, keep your wallet hidden and carry very little of importance. I've heard of unscrupulous guides in the north who demand prepayment for mountain trekking and then just leave you in the woods. Remember never to pay before you have received what you were promised. Thai people are naturally friendly and helpful, but don't get lulled into complacency.

Telephones

The telephone system is new and modern, but it's easier to make an international call than one across the street. Local calls are very time-consuming.

Taxis

Cabs are plentiful and cheap, while Tuk-Tuks are more fun but dangerous. You would think that these three-wheelers would be less expensive, but a normal cab is about the same price. Cabs recommended by hotels have fixed rates and normally have air-conditioning, a nice amenity for those smog-filled days.

Shopping Tips

When shopping, bargaining is the norm, so start at 50% of the asking price and slowly move up (whether it's a cab, a store, or a lady).

Electrical Current

Electricity is 220 volts, but most hotels have lower voltage in the bathroom for your shaver.

Chapter 8

Local Customs

A few tips for an enjoyable stay:

- Buddha images are sacred. Give them respect as you would a piece of furniture in your house.

- The king and queen and the royal family are special. Don't bad-mouth them.

- Dress properly, and take your shoes off before entering a temple of a private house.

- Don't touch a person's head. This is the noblest part of the body.

- Call Thai people by their first name.

- Express your happiness by smiling and you'll receive a beautiful smile in return.

- Intimacy in public is a no-no. Wait until she's in your room. While we're on the subject of customs, I've been told that the two easiest ways to aggravate a Thai are by losing your temper in public, and by publicly showing affection. These are both very true, but what you also want to learn is what a Thai woman is like in private. I had to find that out for myself. Here the words seductive, charming, sexy and submissive take on new meaning.

On a humorous note, don't plan to have your hair cut on a Wednesday, say the Thais. Have it cut on a Sunday to bring you long life. On a Monday, it will bring you health and happiness; and on a Tuesday - power. Never on a Wednesday, for the result will be a disaster! Many barber's shops, especially upcountry, are closed on Wednesday. My favorite day is Thursday when the guardian angels ("Teh-wadas") protect me.

BANGKOK: THE CITY OF ANGELS

Bangkok, formerly "Krugthep," was built along the S-shaped Chao River and established in 1782 by King Rama I as the capital of Siam. After the destruction of the ancient capital of Ayutthaya, in 1767 by the Burmese, the government center was moved to its present headquarters along the river.

For the tourist, Bangkok's central location makes day trips possible to many interesting attractions and local beaches nearby. Bangkokers live in a totally confused state of traffic, noise, and pollution. It's part boom-town, part tradition. The city has the vitality of a child just learning the meaning of uncontrollable growth. It has romance, grace, and charm, most of which are missing in many large capital cities today. Like Los Angeles it has no real city center. Living with ten million people in Bangkok is like getting a taste of strong, old cheese—it may overwhelm you at first, but once you've acquired a taste, other cities may seem lifeless and boring. Here people sing on their way to work, as they get stuck in never-ending traffic. Orange-robed monks beg alms and locals greet you with a smile and a Sawatdee, " good morning."

Above all, Bangkok is a city of contrasts: the rich and the poor, the beautiful and the ugly, materialism and religion, noise and serenity, outlandish sex and prudish morality.

Trying to understand a map of Bangkok can be bewildering. A *Soi* is a lane off a larger road, usually marked by the name of the larger road plus a number. The Soi are numbered consecutively, but with odd numbers branching off one side of the street and even on the other side. The problem is that the *Soi* numbers for odd and even do not progress at the same rate; for instance Soi-20 could be opposite Soi-51. Confused? Don't worry, everyone else is too.

The three basic areas of Bangkok are Siam, Silom-Surawong, and Sukhumvit, but remember, any new street corner could be your center.

Chapter 8

Siam

Surrounding Siam Center, Pratunam, Ratchadamri, and Phloeenchit are the three main streets that make up the biggest shopping district in Bangkok. Here are the large shopping malls and department stores along with commercial complexes. The new 62-story World Trade Center is opposite Ratchadamri Arcade, and if you want to see Thai teenagers at play, Siam Square along with its shopping center is the place to be and be seen. Here are countless upscale coffee houses, bakeries, movie theaters, small boutiques and restaurants to chat the evening away. Nearby are many of the best hotels: the Siam-Intercontinental, the Hilton, the Meridian, the Asia, the Palace, the Regent, and the new Hyatt Regency (formerly Erawan).

Silom-Surawong

During the day, these two streets are the business center for banks, insurance, airlines and other travel companies, retail stores, arcades, and restaurants. On one end is the river, where the **Oriental**, one of the top-rated hotels in the world, sits alongside the **Royal Orchid Sheraton** and the **Shangri-La**. On the opposite end of each street are the Montien Hotel, the Dusit Thani Hotel and the Korean Airlines office (Silom Center).

Patpong is a small area in this district, world famous since the Vietnam War days for all kinds of "entertainment" including the hostess bars surounded by a thieves market, live sex shows, fancy restaurants, and wine and beer bars. Both Thais and foreigners love to live and work here because it provides convenience, status, comfort and excitement.

Sukhumvit and New Phetburi

The first is the longest road in Thailand and leads right up to the Cambodian border, but more important is the fact that Sukhumvit is the way to Pattaya, the famous beach and sex resort. In Bangkok though, the *Sois* branching off the road are where you'll find fashionable residences, apartments, guest hotels, new first-class hotels (like the new and classy Landmark or the Ambassador, the largest in Bangkok), the best girl-watching and procuring clubs, discos and massage parlors. Sukhumvit has both shopping and business sections and some of the sleaziest hotels like the Grace or the Nana and pick-up bars that are centered in Soi Cowboy and the Nana Plaza. The only problem is that to get to the Grand Palace or the River (to cool off or take a boat ride) can be a monumental undertaking, worse than a polluted, one-hour cab ride during rush hour. If you make this trek, I recommend you pay a few extra dollars and take an air-conditioned cab; these deluxe automobiles wait in front of the better hotels.

New Phetburi road is the newly-developed area with the classiest massage centers and bars. Deserted by day, this long street at night is brightened by neon and enlivened by people going out to party and play.

Another interesting area is called **Banglampoo**, which started out as a colorful market and today is one of the world's great travel centers for budget-conscious adventurers. Closer to the Grand Palace area, this is back-packers' heaven, where you'll find most of Bangkok's budget housing and dining, the cheapest travel agents, and pirated cassettes and computer programs.

One last area is **Chinatown**, which is busy and boisterous. Really all of Bangkok is a Chinatown, and these streets around Yaowaraj Rd. have been the largest trading area for the Chinese for the last two hundred years. Not many stay here, but you can spend an enjoyable afternoon shopping in the alleyways, looking for special antiques, or nibbling on cheap snacks.

If you need to exercise, running in Bangkok is not possible. The Siam-Intercontinental does have a short running track, and most hotels have gyms. The only real alternative for a safe and enjoyable run is **Lumpini Park**, between Wireless and Ratdamri in the direction of the Dusit Thani Hotel (I would say East-West, but it would do no good in Bangkok because you can't see the sun due to the smog and haze).

Chapter 8

Another alternative is the **Clark Hatch Athletic Club** which has Cybex, Lifefitness and Startrac exercise machines, an aerobic studio, sauna/steam juice bar, and an outdoor pool. You pay a daily fee for a great way to exercise in this polluted city (231-2250)!

SHOPPING: WHAT TO BUY

One has to remember that all of Bangkok is a shopping center. Around every corner, behind each temple, in all the hotels, and along every major street you'll find someone ready to sell you something. Bargain hard, but ask yourself if you really have a use for the item. Many things, such as the native handicraft, which look so unusual only sit in your closet back home.

Nevertheless, Bangkok is the perfect destination to arrive with *no* suitcase. There are more stores selling garmet bags in Bangkok than girls in the local bars. Prices can be 50% or more off the U.S. prices and selection is unbelievable. Considering the selection of pants, shoes, shorts and shirts in the stores and outside clothes stalls plus their low prices, it makes sense to fill your new suitcase with new clothes.

I usually arrive in Thailand with only a sports bag of clothes for a few days. When I return to the U. S. with all my new purchases, I'm never harassed by custom officials since I only have one suitcase and the clothes inside already have been worn at least once (you're allowed $400 duty free and that would fill five suitcases in Thailand, just don't glamorize your new imitation Rolex watches - copyright infringement is illegal.)

Here are my tips for shopping:

Silk Introduced to the world about forty years ago, Thai silk is hand reeled, hand woven, and hand printed, so it has a natural, uneven look and a coarser texture. The rich colors and designs make Thai silk among the world's finest. The Silom Surawong area is full of shops, and if you don't want to buy silk by the yard (a great buy if you have a friend who can sew), you can purchase scarves and ties as that perfect gift. I recommend **Jim Thompson Silk House**, right around the corner from the red-light section of Patpong on Surawong Road, and **Design Silk** on Silom Road.

Leather There are over 100 tanneries on the outskirts of Bangkok, where hide and leather of high quality are produced. Much of it is sent to the U.S., so you can by-pass the middleman. Most of the stores that sell to the public are located along Sukhumvit Road and its Sois where the best buys are briefcases, large suitcases, bags, and shoes. Here on Sukhumvit are the tailors and booteries that will custom make your order. Watch out for imitation leather. If you're not sure, just hold up a lighted match and watch the shopkeeper run (plastic burns quickly). Also, after I sat on my glasses, I found out this street is great for eyeglasses and quick prescriptions. For one price (under $75, you can get your eyes checked and they will make you two sets of glasses in your choice of frames. Even here you can bargain.

Wood Carving and Silverware Wood carving is an ancient art, practiced in Thailand for seven centuries. Today, most carvings you buy, such as bowls or decorative items, will be for souvenirs since what makes them special is the teakwood. If you have the money and trust your seller, the Chinese-style dining sets in rosewood, inlaid with mother of pearl, are beautiful. Try **Gold Bell Furniture** on Sukhumvit, between Sois 28 and 30. Another great buy is bamboo furniture, but be leery of items that are priced way below comparable items. Shop thoroughly and carefully, and always bargain hard.

Thai silverware is also admired for its elegant craftsmanship. Chinatown is the best place to buy silverware, but I recommend bringing along someone who knows the language and the techniques of achieving rock bottom prices on quality goods. If you're in doubt, just go to the shopping galleries of the Oriental or Sheraton hotels.

Designer Copies Unrestrained by Western copyright laws, these copied goods — like Rolex watches, Lacoste or Fila T-shirts, Gucci leather purses and bags, Christian Dior perfume —are Thailand's best buy. Of course they're illegal, but if you're going to break the law, why not in Bangkok?

Chapter 8

The newest area is Patpong itself, where early in the evening vendors set up booths and stalls to sell the world's best for a pittance, causing many bar owners to complain that all the merchandise distracts their customers. I often buy watches for my friends, but I must admit that there is no way of knowing how long they will last. The latest thing copied is Retina-A, the expensive drug that takes away your wrinkles. Once you take it, you're not allowed much sun. I'd rather have my wrinkles than lose out on watching the bikinis.

A word of warning about copied computer programs: one out of every four cassette tapes that I bought was worthless, and I'd assume the same ratio exists with copied computer programs. See if you can try out your programs before purchasing them and ask for manuals.

Markets

Behind the Indra Regent Hotel is one of my favorite markets, **Pratunam Market**, which is in two sections: a huge covered market for clothes, T-shirts, and original jackets, and a long street of the copy-cat merchandise. For original thick cotton T-shirts, Pratunam Market is the place. However, it gets hot and confusing here, so take a break and have a drink at the Indra Hotel pool across the street, or have your lunch at the cheap food court on the third level of the Baiyoke building across the street. This building is also a condo-hotel from the sixth level up. Underneath is a large shopping complex of original fashions, a movie house, and a snooker club.

If you want to see the rich Thai kids shop, head over to the Siam Shopping Center on Rama IV. Here are four floors of high-fashion clothing that will look good back in the States. If you're hungry, the basements of the large department stores all have food courts, and the **Central Department** store at the end of Silom Road is the best. This store is a multi-level hodgepodge. If you can't find it here, try **Banglampoo Market**, off Chakrapong, where they sell everything from underwear to gold jewelry. The **Weekend Market** at Chatuchak, behind the northern bus terminal, sells clothes, gifts, art-works, you name it, every Saturday and Sunday (7:00 A.M. to 6:00 P.M.) This is Bangkok's best all-purpose market.

WHERE TO STAY IN BANGKOK

According to the Pacific Asian Travel News, there were supposed to be 5,811 new rooms opening in 1991 in Bangkok. A few years ago, due to Thailand's tremendous economic expansion and tourist boom, mostly from Europeans, there was a shortage of rooms during prime season. Now the days of full occupancy are over, and a room glut threatens all the new projects. By the end of 1992 there will be over 18,000 hotel rooms, and the market will be top-heavy in deluxe properties.

This means that you'll be able to have a deluxe room at a budget price. No reason to skimp here, for unlike Rio there are more deluxe properties in Bangkok than in any other place in the world. Another advantage is that most new hotels are part of large chains, so you can shop by toll-free numbers in the United States until you get what you want. Another possibility is to book a cheap room; then,

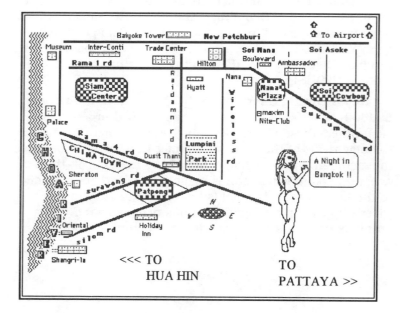

once in Bangkok, go directly to the hotel and negotiate at the front desk; it's a buyer's market. You can also bargain by calling the hotel direct; they're likely giving out big discounts. Remember that prices do not include the 10% service charge or the 11% room tax. If you happen to arrive on Singapore Airlines check their **Stopover Holidays** program which disounts rooms as much as one-third in 41 cities and 28 countries including Thailand.

Hilton An architecturally-pleasing low rise in the embassy part of town. Close to Ploenchit and Sukhumvit roads, with a tennis center and nice gardens. Used by business travelers, so you won't run into any tourist groups, it is rather expensive ($160+) for the location. (800-HILTONS).

Siam Inter-Continental One of my favorite hotels, an oasis in the city. Now 25 years old, it has lost some of its prestige, but its location in Siam Center and its garden complex make it a great buy in the deluxe category. It has an excellent pool and sports facility, plus an interesting lobby, designed the Thai way. My choice for serenity in the midst of chaos. $128+ (800-33-AGAIN).

Dusit-Thani In terms of its location, the best hotel in town. At the end of Silom road and Rama IV, this landmark hotel features luxury rooms and typically Thai good manners. You also get uninterrupted CNN in every room, and its Bubbles Disco is where the wealthy locals hang out. $144+ (800-NIKKOUS).

Royal Orchid Sheraton (800-334-8484) and **Shangri-La** (800-359-5050): Located on the river within a mile of each other, these two modern, high-rise, opulent hotels are the new rivals of the Oriental. I prefer the Sheraton because my membership in its hotel club allows me to book the cheapest room, which still is magnificent, and be upgraded to the best. Also, this hotel is linked by walkway to the River City Shopping Center and has two pools and two tennis courts plus an air-conditioned aerobics studio.

The Shangri-La is the newer hotel with fewer tourists and a glass lobby that reminds one of the Regent of Hong Kong. The perfect place to sip a cool one and watch the river traffic. Both hotels are rated in the World's "top ten" and are a treat within themselves.

Narai Located on Silom Road, halfway between the river and Patpong, Narai is a well-run, budget hotel over 20 years old in the middle of business, entertainment and shopping. The rooms are small, but it has a pool, a great bakery and a pizzeria. $108+ (800-44-UTEL) Up the street is the new Holiday Inn, but who wants to go to Bangkok and stay in a Holiday Inn?

Ambassador The largest hotel in Bangkok, with over 1,000 rooms, 2,500 staff, 13 restaurants, 60 private dining rooms, 50 boutiques, a large pool, a health and tennis club, and a small running track. The Ambassador is located in the best part of Sukhumvit and offers three types of accommodations: Sukhumvit is the cheapest; Main is more expensive; the Tower section, with its great views, is the most exclusive. I've stayed here twice; the place is so big I always get lost. $75+ (800-223-9868).

Landmark Across the street from the Ambassador is the Landmark, a hotel too oriented to serving businessmen. However, if you plan to bring your work with you, you'll enjoy its videotext work terminal in every room. $150+ (800-44-UTEL)

Boulevard 17 Sukhumvit, Soi 17. A budget hotel for businessmen, with a nice pool and brand new rooms, but no frills. $112+ (800-448-8355).

Airport This hotel, which belongs to the Siam Lodge Group (with other hotels in Phuket, Chiang Mai and Pattaya), has a walkway to the airport. For early morning flights, it can't be beat. Also, you can rent a room by the hour for an afternoon snooze if your flight is delayed. A bonus is a massage parlor on the fourth floor where you can pick your masseuse and take her to your room. For $65 (which can be charged to your American Express) you get an hour-and-a-half massage plus you know what (800-448-8355).

Chapter 8

Baiyoke Suite Hotel This is an apartment building, the tallest building in Bangkok, that has been turned into a hotel. It is located behind the Indra Regent Hotel. You get a two-room apartment with an unbelievable view. The pool is small, but outside is the great Pratunam Market. Many five-star hotels will not allow female guests, but at the Baiyoke (255-0330) no questions are asked about overnight friends.

Nana Hotel Located at 4 Nana Tai, a Soi off of Sukhumvit and close to the Ambassador Hotel, this is a great middle-class hotel (252-0121) which gives new meaning to the word *fun*. Not only is the hotel's disco packed every night with lusty amateurs or masage parlor girls with the night off, but the coffee shop is full of ladies trying to stay awake or looking for someone to fall asleep with. Directly across the street is Nana Plaza, a miniature Patpong without the crowds, and down the street is a great massage parlor, Thermae. The hotel is famous for its lack of moral restraint. Ask for the new wing, which has better sound-proofing. This is the only hotel I've stayed at where you can wake up at 2:00 A.M., go downstairs for apple pie, and your doggie bag will include a cute secretary. Bangkok at its raunchiest!

In addition to the hotels listed above, there are countless hotels in Bangkok with no U.S. toll-free numbers. Many are more reasonable than those above and are definitely worth calling. To call Bangkok, dial 01-66-2 plus the seven digit number. Remember, Thailand is one day ahead and 14 hours in advance of Pacific Standard Time.

All hotels have different policies regarding female companions. The best hotels (Oriental or Shangri-La) just don't allow companionship. The next best hotels (Intercontinental, Airport) allow companionship but will charge an extra $20-$50 for an unregistered guest. It doesn't matter if it's for one minute or for the whole night, the price is the same. If you use the hotel's massage service, there is no companionship fee. When you check in, after asking the price of the room, ask about companionship policy.

In all, according to the Tourism Authority of Thailand, the number of new hotel rooms, in major tourist areas, will have increased by 56% in the last four years. All the new hotels are five stars and the word opulent is an underestimate of the grandiose structures! The new Grand Hyatt Erawan, Sukothai, Royal River, Arnoma, Siam City, Tawana Ramada, Imperial, Regent, Menam, Royal Princess, Novotel, Le Merdian President, and The Mansion are a few of the new or remodeled hotels. These are among the best hotels in the world and when they all come on line in late 1992 - early 1993, you can expect a price war. The lobbies, bars and reading rooms provide a wonderful diversion from crazy Bangkok. Here I relax, browse, and pool hop (proper demeanor is to order lunch at a pool if you're not staying at that hotel).

No trip to Bangkok would be complete without a drink at the **Oriental** or **Shangri-La** hotel. My favorite is the Lobby Bar at the Shangri-La; the views of the Choa river are superb and the ambience is royal.

For more details on hotels, sights, transportation, and activities contact: Thailand Tourism Authority, 3440 Wilshire Blvd., Suite 1101, Los Angeles 90010, (213) 382-2353.

WHAT TO SEE AND DO

Sightseeing in Bangkok and its surroundings takes time and patience. You must contend with the heat, the traffic, the foreign language, the hugeness of this city, where nothing is close together. I advise taking tours, with English-speaking guides and hotel mini-vans and delivery.

Few capitals of the world have so many interesting things to see: fascinating klongs (canals), Wats (temples), kick boxing matches, and of course, the one-of-a-kind nightly entertainment that has made this city famous.

Canals If you do only one thing, you must explore Bangkok's waterways. This Venice of the East with intersecting canals, called klongs, up and down the Chao Phrya River, is a mystifying sight. Go down to the pier, either at the Oriental Hotel, which has express boat taxis up to the Grand Palace, or go to the Sheraton and hire a long-tailed boat for about $10/hr. Not only will you see the floating market, along with a million Japanese tourists, where

Bangkok Temple

everyday commerce takes place, but you'll see the side canals where people live, bathe, and eat. The people live in wooden houses on stilts, each with its own spirit house full of the smell of incense and sweet flowers. If it gets too hot, wave over a floating sampan for a frosty one or a snack and then continue your adventure.

You'll stop at the **Royal Barge Museum**, where the royal family keeps its sailing vessels. These boats decorated with unique carvings and intricate gold designs, hold sixty or so oarsmen. As you return to the docks, your driver will rev up that V-8 on a pole and you will fly back at 30 mph.

Grand Palace and Wat Phrakaeo Both of these attractions are located on the same ground in the very heart of Bangkok and can be reached by cab or water taxi. The Grand Palace is famous for its impressive buildings of both Thai and Western architecture decorated with intricate gold carvings embedded with jewels highlighted by turquoise tiles. Notable is the influence of King Rama I's rebuilding of the capital in the image of the ancient capital Ayutthaya.

Among the important buildings are the royal residence pavilion, the disrobing pavilion, the holy water pavilion, the funeral hall pavilion and the coronatiion pavilion.

Wat Phrakaeo is considered the most beautiful of Buddhist temples in all of Thailand. The Wat, better known as the Emerald Buddha, is over two feet high and made of dark green jade. It sits atop a large gold altar with a seasonal cloak that when changed brings good fortune to the new season.

Even more impressive is **Wat Po**, the largest temple in Bangkok. Its reclining Buddha is 140 feet long and 50 feet tall. The feet of the Buddha are inlaid with mother-of-pearl illustrations of 108 auspicious signs of his greatness. On entering these temples I was told I had to wear pants, and just by coincidence there was someone selling pants on the corner. Once inside the temple I discovered that everyone was wearing shorts. I had been had again. Hours are 8:30 A.M. to 11:30 A.M. and 1:30 to 4:00 P.M.

National Museum Just north of the Emerald Buddha is the National Museum, one of the most comprehensive museums in Southeast Asia. Housed in this 18th-century palace are artifacts dating as far back as the stone age. You must see the Thai ceramics, the gold pieces of the princess, the elephant chairs, the royal palanquins and musical instruments from different eras. Don't miss the **Red House**, historically the first living quarters of the royal family, complete with furnishings of the princess Sri Sudarak. Tours available in English, Tuesday through Thursday.

Ancient City Twenty miles outside of the city, near the largest crocodile farm in the world (imagine 30,000 crocodiles crawling around, not to mention snakes), the Ancient City is the creation of a wealthy Chinese immigrant, who tried to reproduce all of Thailand's historical sites in one location. Shaped like a map of Thailand, the park contains replicas of many historical buildings from all over the Kingdom.

Go down to the pier at the Oriental Hotel at 8:00 A.M. and travel up the river of kings into Siam's past, to the ruins of **Ayudhya**, the capital from 1350 to 1767, when the

Burmese leveled it to the ground. It has never been rebuilt. Once it was a city of gilt spires interlaced by man-made canals that carried 200,000 boats a day. Nearby is Bang Pa-In, the new summer palace, architecturally a mixture of Thai, Chinese, Italian Renaissance and Gothic Revival styles. For reservations on this deluxe yacht: 236-0400.

Wat Traimit An astonishing sight, this is the world's biggest gold Buddha image, over 700 years old, weighing over ten tons, near the train station on Traimit Road, and the admission is free.

Rose Garden A great way to escape the noise and the heat. Twenty miles outside of Bangkok, these extensive grounds include a hotel, a boating lake, a swimming pool, bicycles for hire, and traditional cultural performances at 3:00 P.M. daily including dances, Thai boxing, sword fights, and an elephant show. A great place to take your new friend or just to wander around.

Jim Thompson's House Mr. Thompson, who vanished mysteriously in the Cameron Highlands of Malaysia in 1967, was one of the greatest collectors of Thai antiquities. His house is now a museum, just off Rama I Road.

WOMEN AND NIGHTLIFE IN BANGKOK

Bangkok is sexy, lusty, sleazy. The latest report estimates that 20% of the million or so "working girls" in Thailand are foreign and you should have no problem finding someone. Apparently the demand is so strong that the brothel owners bring in girls from Burma and China. This isn't Rio, where girls do it to show off their bodies or make quick "pin" money to add to their income; in Thailand, it's the girl's whole life. It's sad to see these girls with no choice in life, waiting for their next customer. It's amazing that they seem to have fun and put a smile on their faces. Many Arabs and Europeans are known to abuse these girls. As an American you are the preferred customer; many know of girls who went to America during the Vietnam war period and hope that you are kind and generous and maybe will fall in love with them too. (I'm not saying that all Americans are gods when compared to other cultures, as I do know some very sadistic Americans, but in general we seem to fall in love more easily and treat our women as equals.) But in the Orient, women are second-class citizens, often treated in dehumanizing ways. There's nothing you can do to change it, but you can still be one of the kind and generous ones who helps.

Unlike Brazil, in Thailand meeting that special girl takes place only in selected areas. Asian culture defines the woman's role as non-aggressive and submissive. For a woman to be the aggressor indicates sex is a business. This is not to say that you won't fall in love or that you won't get the full attention of a charming Asian lady; it's just that there's no denying the fact that sex is her job.

This is a good time to explain a disease that I, as well as many of my friends, have. It's called *White Man's Fever.* This high-temperature sickness (obsession) simply means that Asian girls drive us totally bananas and we are at their mercy. Yes, these Asian girls know that there are some of us who can't say no to them, and of course they use that to

Bangkok's Patpong Road

their advantage. If you have this disease, or get it on an Asian trip, don't feel guilty or alone—there are millions of us.

The four main areas to go out looking for a woman are massage parlors, brothels, bars, and late-night hang-outs.

Massage Parlors

Thai massage is marvelous. It can last up to two hours and will relax your mind and most of your body for only $10. If you have a weak back or sore knuckles, tell her before she starts. You'll be surprised how many different ways your body can be moved.

Takara, on Patpong 2, offers a good example of traditional massage. Now the other kind of massage is in a totally different environment. It's usually quite easy to tell which kind of parlor you're in; if there is a large glass cage, ten by thirty feet or so, with twenty to forty girls sitting on benches dressed like they're going to the Prom but with numbered badges, then you're in that place where anything goes. Of course, you can still have just a massage here, but the main purpose of the establishment is not to stop there.

Two basic rules: never pay for the whole transaction until it's completed, and don't be afraid to ask the madame for help in your selection. You can walk in, have a beer, and just look, sort of window shopping as I call it, and then leave if you want. If you feel comfortable but can't make up your mind, ask for help. If the prettiest and the youngest are already taken, the madame may recommend someone who is fresh or hard-working. Competition is fierce between the girls, as a pretty lady can make a few thousand dollars a month working ten hours a night, six nights a week. They retire at 25 — who can compete with the new 16-year-olds? — and go back to their village and open a mom-and-pop market with the money saved. Once I met a lady at the Nana Disco, and the next morning she offered to take me to the Rose Garden for the day. She picked me up in her chauffeured new car, but I had to pay for the gas. Figuring she was probably a model, I asked about her job. She said her number was 31 at James Bond Massage.

Sometimes the parlor attendant will demand that you pay up front for the sex, but remember my used-car rule: would you buy this car without driving it first? Since the massage is only a few dollars, let the girl convince you that you want the extras. You negotiate with her directly and it's much more fun when neither of you knows what's going to happen. Once late at night I prepaid and the girl actually fell asleep before the end, and in these places there is no refund for unopened goods.

Another option is to request a body massage in which the girl first soaps you up and then spreads the soap all over with her body. A wonderful experience, and you can ask for two girls to get you extra clean. Again, these massages are cheap and do not require any sex. Any sexual act, oral, manual, insertive, can also be requested; just make sure what your agreed price includes and enjoy.

Some of the better massage parlors are **Mona Lisa** and **Atami** on New Phetchburi Road, **Darling** and **James Bond** on Sukhumvit Road and **La Cherie** in Patpong. Many of the second-class hotels, such as New Fuji at the Trocadero Hotel across from the Sheraton, have small parlors that are friendly and reasonable. Massages in five-star hotels are expensive and unimaginative, but if you check the local papers or the English magazine *This Week*, there are agencies which send over their better employees. It seems that very young girls, who are not dressed properly, have a difficult time getting into nice hotels. Remember, you usually get what you pay for, and nothing is free. If you do make a friend, she would probably like to go out for an after-hour drink and snack. You may find her to be a great tour guide.

Most five-star hotels (like the Intercontinental) have in-house massage service. If you feel lazy and don't want to fight the traffic, noise, and pollution, this service is the practical solution. Remember, you'll pay triple price because it's from the hotel. Once you pick your girl from your hotel's massage parlor line-up, a guard will escort her to your room. The only advantage besides convenience is you don't have to pay an extra "joining fee" that the hotel will charge. Another suggestion is to try the massage parlors in

Chapter 8

lower-class hotels; for example, New Trocadero in the Silam area, where the prices are equivalent to an outside massage parlor but you have the convenience of a hotel room.

Brothels

When you get into a cab or Tuk-Tuk and the driver says, "I have special girl for you," your first instinct is to be suspicious; why should this Thai driver have a girl for me? Actually he's trying to entice you to go to a brothel with him. Not only does he make his cab fare, but he gets a kickback from the brothel's owner. If you do go with him, make sure he understands that you just want to look and are under no obligation to pay for anything other than the ride.

Basically these brothels are no-frill massage parlors with no massage. You enter a hotel room (usually the attendant owns the small hotel) and wait for the parade. After a few minutes ten to fifteen girls come in and sit across the room and stare at you. Usually the girls separate into two groups. Imagine on the left couch several girls ready to give you oral sex, on the right couch several girls ready, but not for *oral* sex. Predictably the old and worn are on the left couch, the young and beautiful on the right. The price is the same with or without (though it may vary from brothel to brothel). Once you take your pick, you pay about $30 to the manager and the other girls leave. Now you have about 30 minutes to take a shower and have sex of your preference. They provide the condom, but I suggest you have an American Latex Prophylaxis. And take another shower. These are village girls from Burma or China who are barefoot and who knows how old. They don't speak any English other than Hi and are as foreign to you as you are to them. If the service is good, tip; if extra special, tip more. These girls live here and are *owned* by the hotel. Your tip is their spending money, so let your conscience be your guide. Your driver will be waiting for you to finish, hoping you had a good time so that you'll tip him too.

If you can remember the location, which is difficult because these brothels are always in some back alley, you can save 20% on your next trip, about what the taxi driver gets as his finder fee. There are probably hundreds of these little brothel-hotels in Bangkok, and each one is a little different. I've heard that some will sell you the girl on a daily fee. One way to rationalize it is to say, if it's not me, then it's the guy behind me, and who's more likely to be the gentler of the two?

The Bar Scene

This is what Bangkok is famous for; Go-Go bars with hot, steamy young ladies dancing around a pole in a little G-string. Each bar has its distinct personality. Just walk up and down the streets and alleys until you see someone you want to meet. Go in and sit down at the bar. The girls eyeball you but leave you alone, trying to figure you out: a loner, a looker, a drinker, a Don Juan (whom they call a butterfly, continually moving on from one of them to the next.) Sooner or later a girl will approach you and ask to sit down. You buy her a drink. Sometimes you'll see someone on stage or wandering around; just give her a friendly smile or stare, and before your next drink arrives, she'll be next to you.

Some bars have hundreds of girls, and it can get quite confusing; since they are all dressed the same, it's simpler to use their number badges to remember a specific lady (all the noise and the smoke certainly don't help). By the way, you need to understand that their custom is that once you buy a girl a drink, you are hers until you leave or you tell her, no more. Make it a rule to pay for each drink, one round at a time. Once the girls realize you're an easy mark for drinks, the line gets very long, for your sweetie may show you off by having you buy her friends drinks, and the bill at the end could pay for your flight home.

It's quite fun going from bar to bar, flirting with some of the most beautiful women in the world and being chased. Thai girls are very good-natured, and just teasing, flirting, singing and drinking is an experience in itself. You don't have to take one to bed to have a good time (the massage parlors are better suited for that), but if the lusty urge arises, it's possible to satisfy it. During your friendly drinking time, the girl's main English will be: What name? Where you from? What hotel you stay? Obviously, the last question is the most important. Many of the better hotels won't allow late-night visitors, and the girls know which can be sneaked into (the lower class hotels thrive on this action and some are more like brothels than hotels).

A friend of mine once became so incensed when he couldn't bring his new love to his deluxe room that he tried to bring her into the Sheraton during lunch time by the back stairs; he still was caught by security. He immediately checked out of his $150 room and checked into the dive next door, figuring he could always be at a Sheraton, but not always would he have the opportunity to be with so many beautiful girls.

In case your hotel doesn't allow guests (your lady will know), there are *always* other possibilities. If you want her to spend the entire night, she will know of cheap hotels. If you just want to satisfy the immediate need, then there are very clean rooms you can rent by the hour. Remember to do all your negotiating before you leave the bar. You must still pay the bar fine. All in all, this can run into an expensive evening, with the drinks, bar fine, taxis, her reward, and the possibility of an extra hotel room charge.

That's why I say that the massage parlors make much more sense. Use the bar scene to find a real girl friend. If you take your time, you can find someone who will move in with you and be your guide and travel companion. Have fun at the bar-hopping game of finding the most perfect girl for you. If you don't find her tonight, there's always tomorrow night. Use the massage parlors or brothels if you can't maintain celibacy.

One of the best bar areas is **Patpong**, the original, 2-block, red-light area in Bangkok. Now it's full of boutiques and booths for imitation Rolex watches or designer goods and bars. Patpong 1 and 2 are the girlie bars, 3 is for the gays and transvestite shows, and 4 is for the Japanese.

Upstairs there are often live shows that are illegal and sometimes raided, perhaps a girl blowing smoke rings with a cigarette in her vagina.

If you need a rest from the madness, between Patapong 1 & 2 is the **Bookseller**, one of the best bookstores in Bangkok, which carries in addition to English fiction, great maps and guides. **Superstar** and **King's Caste** are rated among the top ten bars in the world. In these bars (really discos where only girls in bikinis dance on the stage) you sit back, have a drink, and enjoy numbers 1-100, and if you can't get your favorite's attention by a smile, ask any girl to bring over the number you like. When you buy her a drink (it will be only a few dollars), she's yours until you stop buying her drinks or pay her bar-fine.

If you like getting mauled as you walk in, then try the **Pink Panther** on Patpong 2 across from the Montien Hotel. Upstairs is the most tastefully done live-sex show (if such a thing can be tastefully done) in all of Bangkok. Don't be surprised to see many couples here. There are so many bars, shows, touts, sellers, hawkers and tourists that sometimes a more mellow place is needed to continue the search.

Soi Cowboy, which runs parallel to Sukhumvit Road, between Sois 21 and 23, is the perfect poor man's Patpong. It would seem more proper here to wear cowboy boots and hat, as it does have that laid-back, mid-west feel (sawdust floors etc), even in Bangkok. Not as sophisticated, classy, or expensive as Patpong, but just as much fun. Here there are fewer people, since it's on the opposite side of town and in the middle of nowhere. The prices on everything are lower, and the girls seem younger, more amateurish. The drawback to this long block of bars is the absence of true foxes, who have gone to Patpong for the upscale clientele. **Tilac** seems to be the class bar, and to get you in the mood, **Midnite** has a lingerie show at midnight, when else?

My favorite place is **Nana Plaza**, Soi 4 off Sukhumvit, a block from the Ambassador Hotel and a few blocks from the Hilton and Imperial. Not as raunchy as Soi Cowboy or as crazed, crowded and loud as Patpong, Nana Plaza is a great alternative. I like this area for its options: across the street

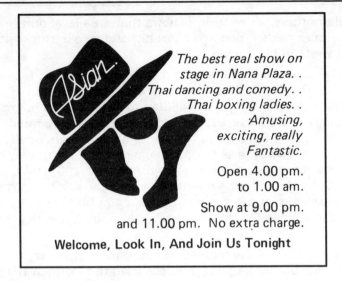

The best real show on
stage in Nana Plaza. .
Thai dancing and comedy. .
Thai boxing ladies. .
Amusing,
exciting, really
Fantastic.

Open 4.00 pm.
to 1.00 am.

Show at 9.00 pm.
and 11.00 pm. No extra charge.

Welcome, Look In, And Join Us Tonight

from the Plaza, a two-story mini shopping mall of bars instead of boutiques, is the Nana Hotel, with a great disco and coffee shop. Up the street is the sleaze hotel, Grace, and its bars. A short walk down Sukhumvit are two great massage parlors; and directly down Sukhumvit toward Soi 1 is the Beer Place Center. The latter is in the Night Bazaar and if this is not enough, across the street, underneath the Boulevard Hotel, is the new German Beer Garden. If you ever wonder what happens to bar hostesses after they reach 25 and haven't made it, this is the place, very friendly. All these hostesses want is for you to pay the bar fine and they'll go back to your room. Inside Nana Plaza the two best clubs are **Asian Intrigue**, with G-stringed Thai boxing ladies, and **Woodstock Rock and Roll Bar**, the best rock and roll till 2:00 in the morning.

My favorite bar? The winner is **Maxim's**, on Soi 4 off of Sukhumvit Rd. Across from the Nana Hotel, make a right (opposite direction of Sukhumvit Rd.) and it's a block down on your left. Upstairs you'll find ten to fifteen beautiful, mellow, a little cultured, and genuinely warm, hand-picked (by the Swiss owner) Thai models. Laid-back, casual, and lots of fun.

Hang-outs

If you haven't found Miss Right yet or you're just plain overwhelmed by the bars, noise, smoke, and the hustlers, head for the hang-outs where you're likely to find amateurs, ladies who have the night off, ladies who simply want to meet a foreigner. My favorite is the **Disco and Coffee** Shop at the Nana Hotel. Good music, food, location, friendly atmosphere. You have to ask the girl to dance, and that's all some want to do. Maybe that's all you want too. The give-away is if she asks where you are staying, hoping it's the Nana, where a quickie is possible. Open at all hours, the coffee shop is where girls get a quick bite to eat, hoping to make a new friend as they build up energy before returning to the dance floor. Be friendly; you never know whom you'll meet. Once I met a madame who was looking for extra girls for her parlor. Apparently a platoon of men had come in and paid the bar fine for most of her girls. She said this was a good place to look for recruits. You can't sell apples from an empty basket, she said. I learned a great deal that day.

If you want to see what attracts Arab men, head over to the **Grace Hotel**, up the street past Sukhumvit. This famous sleaze hotel is unforgettable on a busy night. It's like a Hollywood stage set from the past: chubby little girls with tons of make-up, all wearing mini-skirts, sitting on the laps of their Arab friends. This is not to put down Arabs, for all cultures like their women to have a certain look. The slim, small-breasted, athletic look American men often prize turns off Arab men. At any rate, a trip to the Grace is like entering a time-warp. I consider it one of the main sights in Bangkok. Don't miss it.

At 181 Sukhumvit, up from the Ambassador Hotel, is the Thermae Massage Parlor. Next door is the **Thermae Coffee Shop** which after midnight is packed. Actually it's more of a bar, where everyone stands and checks out the other. Coffee is served. Many different sorts gather around for one last try: the masseuse who has had a slow night, the Go-Go girl with the night off, the secretary looking for some pin money. It's smoky, noisy, and terribly lusty, all those amateurs trying to look pretty and inviting. Here you just walk over and start talking and let nature take its course.

ENJOYMENT PLACE OF CLASS FOR
GENTLEMAN LIKE YOU, WE HAVE GATHERED
VARIOUS TYPES OF ENTERTAINMENT IN ROLLS
CLUB. REWARD YOUR LIFE WITH GOOD THINGS,
TO YOU AND YOUR SPECIAL GUESTS AT ROLLS
CLUB. COME AND FEEL THE GENTLE
ATMOSPHERE....HAVE CLASS

ROLLS CLUB

71 CHAVALIT BLDG, 7th FLOOR
AMBASSADOR HOTEL, SUKHUMVIT RD., BKK.
TEL. 254-0444,
255-0444 EXT. 1131

DREAMS WHICH COME
TRUE. HAPPINESS
WHICH YOU CAN
TOUCH.

Be careful, some of those gorgeous legs are men's, shaved!
Yes, all sorts are here till the wee hours. If you can't sleep,
this is the place to be.

There are so many night time activities in Bangkok.
Perhaps the best method is to find a classy, respectable bar
with English-speaking hostesses and spend time getting to
know someone. Around Patpong these bars are located
upstairs on the back streets. They are often peaceful and
have the prettiest, and most expensive, girls. If you are not
allowed to enter, it doesn't necessarily mean that you're
dressed wrong; it may be a Japanese Only club. Be glad you
can't enter because these are the most expensive drinking
places in Bangkok. Another respectable bar is the **Rolls
Club**, at the Ambassador Hotel. It is more expensive to
drink here than the cheap beers at Soi Cowboy, but the
girls look like models and the ambience is grace and charm.
These are college girls who do speak English and who
would turn any man's head in a American shopping center.
Their motto is "Dreams which come true, happiness which
you can touch." In Bangkok you get what you pay for!

Discos

The discotheque has recently come into its own in
Bangkok. All the latest high-tech gear from abroad has
given each dance floor a "step on the moon" effect. Although many discos cater to the rich Thai kids, it's fun to
watch their fashions and gyrations on the dance floor.
Thousands of the capital's young and trendy show up at
NASA, at 999 Ramkamhaeng Road, on Saturday nights. Up
to 4,000 may be dancing at the same time, and if the wild
atmosphere, the giant wall-videos, and laser light show do
not impress you, then how about a spaceship emerging to
the music of 2001 Space Odyssey as you are bombarded by
balloons?

Of course the classy hotels have European style discos,
but they're not as much fun. The best are **Bubbles** at the
Dusit Thani Hotel, and **Diana's** at the Oriental Hotel. Late
at night the upstairs of Patpong's beer bars turn into loud
discos, and to pass the time you can join in on Happy Hour
on the streets below from 7:00 P.M. to 9:00 P.M. when
drinks are only a dollar or two. The only problem is seeing
all those beautiful girls pile into the Go-Go bars next to you
while you're trying to save yourself for the late-night discos.

For the unusual, try the **Calypso Entertainment Co.** at
Sukhumvit 688, between Soi 24 and Soi 26. Here the
dancers are lovely ..., but they aren't females! This is the
largest transvestite troupe in Asia and one of the best
cabaret shows in Thailand. Twice nightly shows, 8:00 and
9:45.

If you want something more tasteful, try the **Piman
Thai Theatre Restaurant**, at 46 Sukhumvit, Soi 49. During
your meal you will be presented with six Thai classical
performances in ancient costume.

One last idea for different and exciting night life: **Thai
Boxing** takes place in two major stadiums, Lumpini in the
park of Rama IV, and Rajadamnoen on the road by the same
name. Bouts usually begin at 6:00 P.M. every night of the
week and go on all evening. Admission starts at $5. This is
the Thai national sport of agility, their equivalent to baseball, with a long cultural history.

*If you want to experience a night in Bangkok without the 17 hour flight, then a new movie might be appropriate, "**Good Women of Bangkok**". Dennis O'Rourke's documentary follows the plight of a real prostitute ("Aoi") as she wanders the steamy streets, red-light districts, neon bars, and the low-class tourist hotels. The director offered her a rice farm in exchange for real exposure to the black side of life!*

Excursions
in Thailand

If you can take the time to extend your first trip, or if you go back to Thailand more than once, I recommend some excursions outside of Bangkok. Some of these are day trips, while others really need a long weekend or perhaps a week to appreciate fully. Some of these destinations are exotically beautiful, some are blatantly sexploitation, and some are historically and culturally important. Take your choice, but they're all worth it.

PATTAYA

This is most famous beach resort in Thailand, but not necessarily the best. To get a sense of what it's like, imagine all the bars, discos and Go-Go joints of Bangkok, add a few thousand outside beer halls filled with young girls, a dozen or so massage parlors, a few gay clubs and hordes of Europeans, and now you'll have the picture. This is probably the most decadent place on earth where the norm is drugs, pimping, and sex-tours (busloads of European, Arab, or Japanese men being dropped off in front of massage parlors and unzipping their pants in unison). It does have some of the best hotels in Asia at great prices, and it's only two hours by bus from Bangkok. It also offers excellent facilities for water sports, golf, tennis, and hiking.

Pattaya, which is their word for the wind when it blows from the southwest to the northeast at the beginning of the rainy season, used to be a sleepy fishing village until the first American servicemen arrived in 1961. Since then it has become the premier beach resort in all of Asia, now called the Thai Riviera. You can find great shopping, food and sports, but its claim to fame is sex for sale.

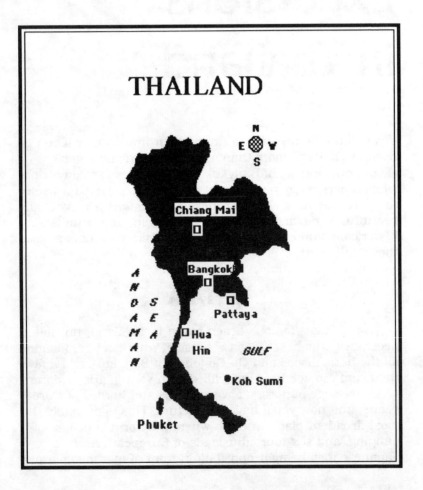

Central Pattaya Road is a long strip of hotels, stores, and bars with no redeeming qualities other than bargain prices. It's not that I'm downgrading Pattaya, but there are so many great beaches, mountains, and ancient relics to see in this wonderful land that to spend much time in a city designed for one purpose seems ludicrous. For example, there is a deserted and truly beautiful island off-shore, Koh Samet (not to be confused with Koh Sumui, the new hot spot discussed below - its Samui or Sumui depending on your guide or map), which makes this trip worthwhile, but if you're short on time, there are better places to visit and explore.

WHERE TO STAY

Right outside of Pattaya there is an excellent, full-service hotel, the **Royal Cliff**, with its own beaches and a Royal Wing with its own pool and opulent suites. 700 rooms, 9 restaurants, 4 bars, 6 tennis courts, a shopping village, three golf courses nearby, and even an elevator to the beach. (280-1737.)

One advantage to staying right in Pattaya are the cheap hotel prices. Because of the bad publicity and overbuilding, this area has some of the best hotel deals in all of southeast Asia. If Bangkok sounds crazy, polluted, and expensive, then I suggest a stay in Pattaya area. Only a few hours from the airport (depending on traffic and mode of transportation) and you can expect hotel rates 50% less than Bangkok. This is a great place to recoup from that twenty-hour flight and get yourself organized.

In town I like the **Orchid Lodge** because it's just a little north of the craziness of the main strip and it's in a garden setting with tennis courts, animals roaming around, and an Olympic pool. From Bangkok you can book this hotel at 429-901. If you're wondering why this phone number has only six digits, it's because local Thai cities have six-digit phone numbers whereas the capital has seven.

Chapter 9

Across the street is the best hotel in town, the **Dusit Resort**, which used to be the old Grand Palace Hotel. This unique nine-story hotel fronts two semi-private beaches with a free-forming pool that makes you feel you're going to fall into the ocean.

Another good choice is the totally remodeled **Royal Garden Resort**—your choice of high-rise or bungalow units, centrally located and the nicest pool in town (428-122).

There are hundreds of other hotels to choose from, so if you want to make this an extended sex-and-sun vacation, spend a day checking out the hotels individually. When you are in Bangkok, read the English papers for the newest promotional prices. With a little luck, a few phone calls and patience you'll find that ocean front penthouse with a million girls to keep you occupied. Culture this is not, but for a few days it's certainly fun.

TRANSPORTATION

To get to Pattaya from Bangkok, you take the northern bus terminal.

Within the city, as in most small Thai cities, such as Chiang Mai and Patong Beach, if you want to go from your hotel to a bar, flag down (just raise your finger) the Toyota mini-trucks with rear bench seats and tell your driver where you want to go. If you're not sure where you want to go, just ring the bell above you and he'll stop and let you off and tell you how much you owe him. If you know where you're going, it's a good idea to negotiate the price before you jump in. Pay as you leave, and watch how much the guy in front pays. Look like you know what you're doing, or the driver will try to charge you double. Either way, it's the difference between one dollar and two for a half-hour trip.

WHAT TO SEE AND DO

While you're there, if you want to hear the latest disco, massage, or bar info, turn to the rock radio station 107.75. All the action is concentrated on a narrow boat-shaped beach strip divided into four segments - North Pattaya, the village, the cliff, and the offshore islands.

The village of Pattaya in the south is the center of carnal activity. Some people call this the "Patpong" of Pattaya. Here you'll find all the beer bars, steamy night-clubs, the **Pattaya Palladium** (the largest disco in southeast Asia) and a host of transvestite cabaret shows with the ones at Alcazar and Tiffany's the best. A special note should be given to the **Marina Bar and Disco**. This is Pattaya at its best: the bar is a unique complex of Thai boxing, snake shows, giant wall videos and at prime time (say 11:00 P.M. or later) up to 1000 girls looking for a partner. An unbelievable sight!

On my last trip I was accompanied by my best male friend. As I showed him the newest hotels and local sights on a evening stroll (he hates these inspections) he vanished. Appearing a day latter he explained he was kidnapped by two girls, abused repeatedly, and only returned to re-supply with American prophylactics! This is the "wicked " city of the east.

BAR SURVIVAL

Bars, discos, and a-go-go places (where girls dance in bikinis on a stage, hoping you'll call their number), all work the same way in the tourist resorts. A-go-go bars open around 9:00 P.M. but the beer bars start around noon. Remember, a-go-go girls and beer-bar girls do not like each other. It's like putting a cat and a dog together in the same room. A-go-go girls feel they are high-class, demand more money,

order more drinks, but are much prettier. Beer-bar girls are jealous of the fancy a-go-go girl. Take your pick, but don't mix.

A last suggestion: as on our used-car lot, the best go first. If you must have the prettiest a-go-go girl, get there at 9:00 P.M. when they open. Many times groups of men on sex-tours will come in and take all the pretty girls. When in Thailand, settle all financial dealings before you leave the bar. The best way to picture the situation if you don't do it this way is to imagine you're returning a rental car and the counter person starts adding up all the extras that you weren't informed of before you took delivery.

OUTSIDE PATTAYA

My favorite place to gather energy and my senses is the **Wong Amat Hotel**. The Wong Amat is a complex of low rise units on 20 acres of landscaped tropical gardens, with over 200 rooms including chalets and bungalows. Set on Pattaya's northwest side with its own private beach and away from the commotion of sin city, this is Pattaya at its quietest (Fax 66-038-428599 or call direct 66-038-426999).

Another possibility is **Jomtien Beach**. This is Thailand"s fastest growing resort area (on the far eastern side of Pattaya, an extra half-hour cab ride) with miles of sand and peaceful surroundings. The focal point is the new **Ambassador City Hotel** with 2,500 rooms and a lavishly equipped health farm and fitness center (038-231501).

CHIANG MAI

If you're looking for a land of beauty, hospitality and good manners, plus mist-shrouded mountains and fertile valleys, then Chiang Mai is for you. The second largest city in Thailand, the "Rose of the North," it is situated in a high valley at the foot of the majestic Doi Suthep mountain and has a refreshing, cool climate and a peaceful atmosphere. It has become a fast-developing tourist center, famous for its hilltribe treks, ethnic handicraft, and over 300 ancient temples. There are German beer parlors and European restaurants now, but it still has a village serenity.

Chiang Mai has its own dialect, costumes, dances, and cuisine. Today the city is actually two cities: the old 13th-century village with a moat and thick walls for protection, and the new city with fancy restaurants and boutiques spread all around the old city, between its moat and the river, as well as across the river on the east bank. This is a good place to shop for fine silk and nielloware.

Thai Airways offers several daily flights and a new non-stop to Hong Kong. As for transportation in town, there are *samlors* (pedicabs) and *tuk tuks* galore. If you are really adventurous, you can rent your own bike and pedal around the fascinating square moat or down to the Mae Ping river.

In Chiang Mai there are three seasons: rainy from June to October, hot from March to May, and cool and refreshing from November to February. There are 1,2205 Wats (monasteries) in the area, but the real claim to fame is the graceful, attractive women that inhabit the city. In the bars and brothels are some of the most beautiful Thai women. This certainly adds excitement to this mountain city, and the completion of new hotels makes a visit to Chiang Mai a true pleasure.

The newest and best place to stay is the **Rincome Hotel**, with 160 rooms, two pools, and spacious gardens, trees, and flowers. (From Bangkok, call 252-6045, or from the U.S., 800-448-8355.) A good second choice is the **Novotel Hotel**, right in the middle of the action on Changklan Road, the main drag for bars, food, and parties. Here is a gym and deluxe rooms. (From Bangkok, call 234-1666.) One last possibility is the **Mae Ping Hotel**, just a block away from the famous Night Bazaar and Mercedes limousine service (053-270160).

As with all your trips in Thailand, your local travel agent can make all your reservations for you, but try to pay one night at a time, for sometimes you get put in the worst rooms when you prepay an entire trip. Keep your schedule free enough to shop around if you're not happy with your hotel.

HUA HIN AND KOH SUMUI

These are two of the better beach resorts that will make your trip enjoyable and also allow you to explore different environments: one is noisy, the other peacefully aristo-cratic.

Hua Hin is a small fishing port about 120 miles south of Bangkok. To get there while you're in Bangkok, you take a cab to the southern bus terminal and buy a ticket for the hourly air-conditioned buses. This was Thailand's first real beach resort and has been the Thai royal family's summer residence since Rama IV built his palace here in the mid-1920s. This villa is actually a compound of bungalows with a Victorian gazebo in the midst of a scenic group of rocks near the village. The elite of Thailand used to spend the hot months of March and April here, but today it's a middle-class family retreat with lots of charm despite its average beach. Everywhere are signs of the royal past, from the old-fashioned deck chairs on the promenade, to the royal waiting room shaped like a Thai palace at the railway station, to the clipped topiary gardens in the old Hua Hin Hotel.

Besides some unusually good hotels, this is the perfect spot for travelers who are tired from touring the Wats, checking out the a-go-go's, and dealing with the traffic and the noise. There are no bars here, but in town (a short walk or quick tuk-tuk ride) you can buy flowers for the amateur girl singers and if you buy enough they come over to express their thanks. Apparently the cut they get of the flowers sold during their performances is the main source of their income. The only problem is if you're too generous, all the girls expect your patronage, and when you don't buy they give you dirty looks. I guess they feel you don't like their singing. A delightful way to spend an evening and make friends.

Aside from the town, the good restaurants, and the three-mile sandy beach, there's not much to do here, but that's why you come. The **Royal Garden Resort** is the best hotel, with 217 ocean-front rooms and full water sports. (From Bangkok, call 255-8822.)

North of Hua Hin is **Cha-Am,** a Thai-style beach resort with old wooden houses that face the beach and modern bungalows for experienced travelers. Twenty years ago it was mostly bush and desert sands, but today it has **The Regent** (from Bangkok, 251-0305), a stunningly beautiful hotel that rivals the best of Pattaya. Here you'll find three different styles of accommodations, the Regency Wing (total deluxe), standard hotel rooms, and beach front cottages. A just opened **Melia Hua Hin** (a Spanish hotel chain in Thailand) is the newest and flashiest. It encompasses 297 high rise rooms, tennis courts, free-form swimming pool, fitness center, horseback riding and even a children's club. A bonus is that it's close to two golf courses and the one of the nicest beaches in the area (032-511-053).

South of Hua Hin is a new "all-inclusive resort," called **Club Aldiana Siam.** Situated on a beautiful beach, this resort includes buffet meals, all sports, jazz dance, legitimate massage, sauna, and a dinner show every night with your room rate. (662-233-2151).

Koh Sumui, an island about 450 miles south of Bangkok in the Gulf of Thailand, used to be the backpacker's dream: a tropical paradise of green hills and coconut groves, huge palm trees swaying over the golden sand, and rustic bungalows surrounded by open-fire fish restaurants that serve famous magic mushroom omelets. This deserted, hard-to-reach island was the perfect dream hideaway. But a few years ago, the airport opened and everything changed. First came electricity, then the dirt bikes (with no mufflers), then the discos and German beer bars, and finally the first-class hotels.

The two main beaches, **Lamai** and **Chaweng**, are major tourist centers now with pick-up bars, touts, and noise pollution. This is not to say the island has lost its charm, as you can hike to waterfalls or lush mountain tops, motorbike around the island in two hours, and eat exotic fish with the

Chapter 9

locals, or just kick back on the beach. When we arrived during Christmas season (January to June is dry and hot, and July to November carries a chance of rain), we had to beg for a hotel room, but our mini-bus driver kept on trying different places until he found us a vacancy. The people are kind and helpful, but I'd get there before tourism spoils it.

Koh Sumui has a sister island with no development yet, Koh Pha-Ngan, just a short boat ride away. Bangkok Airways has daily flights now (253-4014), but if you are going during high season, make your reservation far in advance.

The charm of Koh Sumui goes back 1500 years when fishermen sought refuge here from the strong winds of the gulf and found the soil fertile, the squid and other seafood plentiful, and the bay protected and beautiful. In the early 1980s this coconut-palm tree paradise became the destination of world travelers and backpackers. Over the years the word leaked out about this thatched-roof, bungalow-lined heaven. Sumui's beaches are famous for their beauty and long curves of pure white (and sticky) sand. Chaweng Beach is the biggest, but Lamai is where the action is. This singles-oriented beach isn't great for swimming, but it does have an interesting village of bars, discos, and restaurants.

If you don't have much time, I prefer Phuket, for as different and lush as Sumui Island is, it isn't made for the middle-aged American male. It's certainly fun and laid-back, but it's a young person's adventure paradise. Once the development becomes more organized and more traditional entertainment arrives, I think its market will change too. This is now what I call a cheap-thrill resort: low priced accommodations (the nicer ones are secluded), with cheap food and entertainment. At night, before the discos start (the best being the Flamingo), everyone has dinner at a favorite video bar (you choose your restaurant by what video is showing) and prepare for the good times.

It's considered normal to move from one beach to another. Fat Mama, who ran the **Weekender Villa** on Lamai Beach, treated us like royalty even though we had bungalow rooms. She even drove us to the airport in her new BMW (business must be great) when our ride didn't show up. Chaweng Beach is more mellow and has many more couples and tour groups. This is one resort where you must rent a bike for transportation; remember, they drive on the left and are crazy, so find a helmet.

If you must have the largest swimming pool on the island, then try the **Hilton Garden Resort**. A little south of Lamai beach, this resort has forty deluxe rooms, all with air-conditioning (077-272-22). The most deluxe property on the island is called **Sumui Euphoria**. All rooms and beach front suites have views of Pha-Ngan island and the hotel has one of the few tennis courts on the island. A five-star resort for those of you who just want to disappear (662 - 255-7901).

Before leaving you must confirm your ticket back to Bangkok or they will cancel you. Since there are no telephones, you must pay a travel agent (and give him your ticket) to reconfirm for you, a real pain.

PHUKET:
THE BEST BEACH RESORT IN THE WORLD

I rate this beach resort number one in the world! No other beach resort has more to offer: crystal clear waters, fourteen different beaches, silky sand, a multitude of water and land sports, lush mountains, jungle-like parks, uninhabited caves for exploring, off-shore and remote islands, a unique capital city full of nightlife and sights, some of the best hotels in the world, a new international airport, and loads of beautiful women.

The largest island in Thailand, Phuket lies some 580 miles south of Bangkok in the Andaman Sea. The word *"Phuket"* comes from the Malaysian word Bukit, which means mountain. From a distance Phuket looks like a mountain rising from the sea.

In 1960, Phuket barely had roads across it; now it is the jewel in the crown of Thai tourism and has the highest per-capita income of all the provinces in Thailand. The main city, Phuket Town, located in the southern quarter of the island, is the business and transportation center. Its Sino-Portuguese style architecture comes from the explorers and the local Chinese inhabitants three centuries ago. In 1557, the Portuguese on one of their voyages for new world treasures, came to this island and found a seaport trading in rhinoceros horn, ivory, gems, and pearls. At the beginning of the twentieth century, Phuket was a bustling trade center with tin, rubber and pearl farming as major exports. Phuket has an enormous deposit of quality tin, and even today elephants bring the ore to the towns to be smelted.

The main town has a relaxed pace and some traces of the prosperous past; grand homes of the tin and rubber millionaires are still present. Ask to be dropped off in front of the "Pearl" hotel and your city center (what the Patong

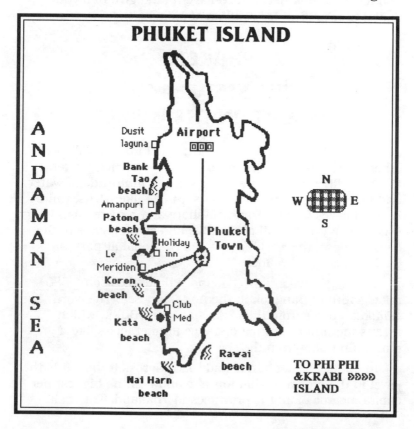

PHUKET ISLAND

ANDAMAN SEA

Dusit laguna

Airport

Bank

Tao beach

Amanpuri

Patong beach

Holiday inn

Phuket Town

Le Meridien

Koren beach

Club Med

Kata beach

Rawai beach

Nai Harn beach

N
W   E
S

TO PHI PHI
&KRABI ᗡᗡᗡᗡ
ISLAND

Beach area lacks in means of massage parlor's is found at the Pearl Hotel -in the basement called "Madam's"). For dinner try **Joy Restaurant** and shop the adjoining night bazaar.

A bonus to this location (a short cab ride from city center) is that you're on "Poonphol" road and its surrounding Soi's (side streets). Here you'll find countless good-time bars that cater to your lusty after meal treat. These are the bars the Thai men visit to satisfy their biological need and are half the price of a massage parlor. Just walk in, order a coke and pick a girl. Once selected (there are 20-30 bars all with 10 to 50 girls waiting to serve you) she takes you to her own room and does whatever you ask! Granted these aren't "Miss Thailand" contestants but the fun is spending an evening just walking the streets and window shopping.

To get home to Patong beach it is suggested to take a small pick-up (will hire out as a cab for you) since the hour will more than likely be late (lusty window shopping time seems to go by so fast).

ARRIVING AT PHUKET AIRPORT

The airport, in the northern sector, is international and efficient. A new runway will be operational in 1992, with all international arrivals having brand-new facilities and walk-through ramps. With over half a dozen daily flights on Thai Airways and a short one-and-a-half-hour flight from Bangkok, Phuket is an easy place to get to (during the high season, Thai Airways flies 400-hundred-passenger Jumbo Jet 747s on this popular route). New international routes have just opened: Trade-Winds Air, an affiliate of Singapore Airlines; Dragon Air, an affiliate of Cathay Pacific (flying Cathay Pacific from the United States allows frequent flyer mileage credit on American Airline's club); Malaysian Air, and Thai Airways International have flights. Direct, non-stop connections to Phuket are now available from Hong Kong, Singapore, Taipei, Kuala Lumpur, and Tokyo. There is no need to go through Bangkok. If you happen to be in Europe, LTU (German airline) has started non-stop service from Dusseldorf and Munich - too bad it's not from Los Angeles or San Francisco.

Chapter 9

My favorite connection is **Singapore Airlines** non-stop flight (SQ#5) from Los Angeles to Taipei that leaves at 1.00 A.M. and arrives in Taiwan at 6.30. A.M. the next day. The flight on China Air (CI#645) or Thai Air (TG#619) leaves for Phuket at 10.00 A.M. and arrives at 1.30 P.M. If you want to save some money you can purchase the entire ticket on China Air with a free hotel night included (CI#005 leaves Los Angeles at 2.00 P.M. and arrives Taipei at 8.00 P.M. the next day). It is always cheaper to purchase one ticket with the same airline than break up carriers - you pay for convenience.

If your travel agent tells you there is a direct flight to Phuket from Los Angeles — don't believe it! Thai International promotes a direct flight, TG #771/TG#241, but it leaves Los Angeles at 11.35 A.M. and arrives Bangkok 10.30 P. M. the following night! Your flight to Phuket doesn't leave till 7.45 A. M., which means a seven hour wait after customs. You can do just as good through another Asian Hub that has non-stop flights to Phuket.

WHERE TO STAY

Once you land, hop on a minibus to your hotel and enjoy paradise. Remember, go directly to **Patong Beach** and make Phuket Town a separate tour. Patong Beach is Phuket's foremost beach resort. Its natural beauty, two miles of white sandy beach, clear turquoise ocean water, soft breezes, and fantastic underwater sealife make this the perfect spot.

There is quite a range of accommodations (simple bungalows to five-star hotels and deluxe condos), as well as an exciting nightlife (bars, a-go-go dance halls, discos). This beach village is about ten miles outside the city and has great beaches to the north and south of it. The best hotels here are the ocean-front **Holiday Inn** (from Bangkok, 236-7245), or next door the **Merlin**, with 180 delightful rooms set among palm trees with informal, tropical architecture; **Coral Beach** on 68 acres on the south end (from Bangkok, 256-9317), and the new elegant, 40-story **Royal Paradise** (from Bangkok, 255-3784). My favorite is the **Club Andaman Beach Resort**, a short walk from the main action center, with two pools, tennis courts, and high-rise suites or inexpensive bungalows (from Bangkok, 270-1627, or fax direct 66 76 321527).

If you must be in the center of the action and on the beach, I suggest **Patong Beach Hotel**, which has not only the newest, ocean-view rooms but also the most popular disco, **Banana**, in all of Phuket (Bangkok reservation number 233-0420 or Fax direct 076 321 541). If you want deluxe accommodations with a little privacy, then I would suggest **The Residence Kalim Bay**. All the units are privately owned two-bedroom Thai styled condominiums (with on-site international management - they even have an office in Westlake, Calif; 805 499-8590)) that include all deluxe amenities with full kitchens and unobstructed ocean views.

If you arrive during off-season (high season is November 15 through March 1), you won't need a reservation. A good place to be dropped off would be the Holiday Inn, centrally located on the beach. To the left or right, you may choose from among several large hotels or many intimate bungalows if the Holiday Inn isn't for you. The manager of the Holiday Inn sometimes rents out his private unit at the Kalim Bay Hotel and the front desk gives special rates for extended stays. This condominium hotel is a few miles north of the main beach with easy taxi access (Fax 66- 76- 321307 or phone 76-3211456).

If there is one disadvantage to this island, it's the weather. The monsoon (wind and rain) season lasts six months of the year (May to October). The good news is that hotel rates drop 50%, and there are some days of sun mixed in with the rainy ones. Early November or April is the perfect time to miss the crowds and still be guaranteed lots of sun. It's always warm: just picture a Caribbean island with Thai food, culture and charming women.

If you must stay in town, the newest and best is the **Metropole Hotel** (076-215-050). Or in town, the most fun and centrally located hotel is the **Thavorn Hotel**, on Rasda

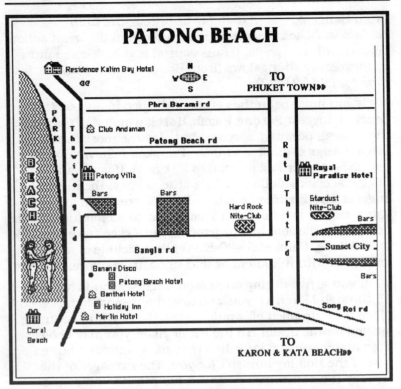

PATONG BEACH

Rd. Besides a swimming pool, game room and tour counter, it has a swinging disco for late-night play (from Bangkok, 245-0189).

Don't panic for fear of not getting a nice hotel room in the "best beach resort in the word." According to a June 1991 survey by the Tourism Authority of Thailand, between 1991 and 1994, at least 14 new hotels will open, adding 2,558 rooms to the present total of 12,477. Besides these new 5-star properties, there are countless bungalows, guesthouses, and lodges opening daily.

From Patong Beach there are three methods of transportation to town: a rented bike or car (not recommended - lots of crazy drivers and over a steep hill), join a mini-bus that gathers passengers in front of the Merlin Hotel (beach side), and my favorite mode - the free shuttle from the Merlin (lobby side) to its sister city in town - " The Phuket Merlin."

Beyond Patong Beach

Just a mile over the hill from Patong Beach is another beautiful beach, **Karon Beach**. On the way you pass the deluxe **Le Meridien Hotel** with its own beach, two swimming pools, a tennis club, a shopping arcade, a disco and over 470 rooms (from Bangkok, call 254-8147). Karon Beach is bordered by long-needle pine trees which separate the marshland from the sea. The three-mile beach is breathtaking but development has started, and huge resorts have just been completed. A new shopping center, Karon Shopping, now has beer bars and rock-video restaurants for entertainment. One of the newest hotels is the ultra-modern **Arcadia Hotel**, with 250 rooms directly across from the middle of the beach (from Bangkok, 254-0921). Directly on the beach is **Karon Villa**, with ocean-front suites or a bungalow compound. This is my choice because of its perfect location for shopping and activities and its ocean-front pool (from Bangkok, 251-8491). Separated by a rocky promontory is **Kata Beach** and its little sister, **Kata Noi**. Kata Beach is only a few miles down from Karon and has a double-curved bay with rocky headlands at each point. A low, rounded hill of rock topped with evergreen trees divides the two beaches. Here is where **Club Med** built its new resort; from Bangkok you can book the Cub Med as a hotel with one to seven night stays (from Bangkok, 253-0108). On Kata Noi the only hotel is the **Kata Thani Hotel**, where you can choose a seaside bungalow or the three-story hotel and enjoy one of the nicest beaches in all of Asia complete with 3 restaurants, two huge pools, a tennis club and water sports (from Bangkok, 252-6045 or from the U.S. 800-448-8355).

You'll need to arrange for transportation around the island, as there is much to see and do. You might rent a motor bike or a jeep to traverse the dirt roads. A hotel manager explained to me that three people a day die from traffic accidents on the island and it seemed that he had to go to a funeral every month for someone from his work force. So be careful, and don't assume that the other driver is looking out for you. Remember, Buddhists believe in an afterlife.

Chapter 9

Karon Beach

Some of the other hotels in the more unusual areas are **Phuket Yacht Club**, perched above a beautiful beach of Nai Harn, looking down on its own Chinese junk parked in the bay (from Bangkok, 214-4020); the **Dusit Laguna**, a member of the famous Bangkok chain, situated on the northwest coast in secluded Bang Tao bay. Complete with graceful gardens, a waterfall, two lagoons, and 240 tastefully decorated rooms (from Bangkok, 233-1130); **Pearl Village Hotel**, located amidst tropical foliage and animals (from Bangkok, 260-1022); and the **Amanpuri**, a super-deluxe property of 40 individual suites in the ultra-exclusive bungalow set at Pansea Beach, with its own yacht anchored at Surin Beach. The Amanpuri's chauffeured Volvo 740 picks you up at the airport. Spoil yourself in this magical place (from Bangkok, 250-0746).

If for some reason you get bored in Phuket, then you could head out to **Koh Pi Pi** Island, where there are sensational beaches and new resorts. The island is so narrow it seems you could hop over it. There are long beaches on both sides and a village hotel. On the way to **Krabi**, the upcoming resort which I plan on visiting soon, you can stop at **Phang Nga**. This island is famous for its weird, limestone formations rising out of the sea like grim guardians of an ancient civilization. The James Bond movie "The Man with the Golden Gun" was shot in this spectacular bay. Some other excursions are Coral Island (for swimming, fishing, snorkeling, and sunbathing), Pi-Pi Island (beautiful cliffs rising from the sea, surrounded by colorful coral, and caves with ancient wall paintings), and a sightseeing tour of the city (including Phuket Hill with its view of Phuket Town, Wat Chalong, a 100-year-old Buddhist temple, and the Marine Biological Research Centre and Aquarium).

For the underwater nature lover, there is the **Similans Islands** – about 60 miles northwest of Phuket. These islands are a marine natural park and are considered to have the best underwater scenery in Asia plus pristine white beaches and coral reefs. The real fun is getting there by a jet catamaran, the "Jet Cat." The high speed Norwegian Cat covers the distance in 150 minutes!

NIGHTLIFE IN PHUKET

You won't be disappointed in Phuket. Patong Beach is full of beer-bars, discos, and a-go-go bars. The best of the a-go-go bars is called **Rock Hard** (on Soi Bangla, which is the main artery to the beach). The main beach road, called Thavee Wong Road or simply "Beach Road," turns into a one-way street at Bangla Road. This road also contains hundreds of beer-bars, all with anxious ladies waiting to serve you a drink. Across from **Doolie's Place** (where Rock Hard nite club is upstairs) is the newest beer bar, disco, nite club entertainment complex — **Sunset City**, in which **Stardust** is the best.

A girl from Rock Hard will cost around $50 for the evening (always negotiable) and a bar-fine of $12. Remember, a good hotel will charge an extra $20 for a lady to join you, and she must leave at 7:00 A.M. unless you register her to your room. Don't do this, for then she has access to your room key. Remember the saying, marry an ugly girl. The beer-bar girls, though not as pretty or as fashionably dressed, are half the price and usually become good friends. If you make it beyond 12:00 midnight, head to Banana's Disco at the Patong Beach Hotel for one last look. After midnight, a-go-go girls, beer-bar girls, amateur hustlers and female Japanese tourists make this disco a man's dream. If you want to dance, just walk onto the dance floor and dance close to the lady that interests you (most girls dance with themselves, and it's not necessary for a man to ask a woman to dance).

One of the more amusing sights takes place early (around 6.30-7.30 A.M.) each morning. As I go for my run (I'm a morning person) there is a parade of young Thai girls, dressed to the hilt and holding their high heels, slowly walking home. This is the time they must leave their "new love" for the hotel policy is that they must depart before the general hotel populace awakens (better hotels only). This way the hotel makes money both ways: charging an extra joining fee for the lady yet keeping its good image as a family resort.

If you are looking for a physical workout, not of the fleshy kind, I suggest the Holiday Inn. A fully-equipped gym and professional trainers are included in the entrance fee. This is a great place to make new friends from different countries and meet legitimate vacationing females whom you might convert into bad girls.

Koh Pi Pi Island

Bar Choices Patong Beach

It's obvious why I like Phuket so much and return year after year. I feel sorry for all of those men who go to Hawaii or Cancun and think that they have been to a fun beach resort. For only a few hundred dollars more they could be in a true paradise. Admittedly, the flight would be longer, but picture a pristine Caribbean island with grand hotels - sports - food - entertainment - sights and an unlimited supply of beautiful women.

For any explorations in Thailand, I recommend that you deposit your purchases at the inexpensive storage facilities at the airport and travel as lightly as possible. Simply retrieve your goods at the airport before boarding your return flight. The less you carry, the simpler it is to travel.

Once you've returned home a strange metamorphose will have occurred. You'll be friendly, out-going, flirty, and have the aura of confidence. It seems once you get used to beautiful women they become more aware of you! No more will that girl on the life-cycle or aerobic class (the one you've been meaning to talk too for the last six weeks) remain unaware of you. Your only problem will be which one to flirt with first.

EPILOGUE

Traveling is a learning experience, and one of the greatest lessons is that you finally understand that mystifying word: APPRECIATION. It's like you never missed your mom, your cat, your favorite television show, the freeway, the supermarket, or your own toilet seat until you don't have it anymore. Once you return from a journey, you really appreciate what you have and finally understand what most people live without. Now that boring and uneventful life of yours isn't so bad.

Rarely does one return from a trip a superficially changed man. What changes is the way you perceive, appreciate, and respect the world around you. Yes, there are days of travel in which you might eat alone and not talk to a soul. More than likely though, half the time you'll meet people who are interesting, beautiful, fun, and creative. You will learn about their culture, their foods, their music. You will see how the other half lives. You will learn to respect what is different about their world. You will come to understand why the rest of the world envies, and sometimes hates, the American. We do have the best of everything.

This knowledge doesn't come knocking at your door; you have to go out and find it. The risks of embarrassment, loneliness, and discomfort are great, but the rewards are far greater. Now I know I'm the luckiest person alive and I fully appreciate it.

210

APPENDIX

SEXUAL DISEASES, AIDS, AND OTHER HAZARDS

I firmly believe it's more dangerous to drive on the L.A. freeways than to play around a little in a foreign country. The trick is to maximize your rewards while minimizing your costs. This doesn't mean abstaining from sex, but going about it in an intelligent and thoughtful manner.

If you play, use a latex condom with a water-based lubricant, American style, with nonoxynol 9. This chemical has been shown to kill HIV. Don't use an oil-based lubricant (for that "Virgin Mary") as Vaseline or whatever the oil is will destroy the condom. The failure rate is directly related to non-proper use. A forgotten practice is how to put a condom on! If you have any doubts, *read the instructions!*

Also, avoid anal or tissue-tearing rough sex, refrain from sex with a partner who shows signs of drug use, take showers both before and after sex, and spend some time with a new lady before you get intimate. Look at it as an investment; minimize your risks, maximize your rewards. It is really best to have some idea whom you're dealing with.

My worst fear is not getting AIDS or some weird disease from sex, but getting seriously injured in a car accident in a foreign country and needing an operation. Blood donors in foreign countries are not screened as thoroughly as they are in the United States. In some foreign countries like Brazil and Spain, blood banks are riddled with blood from low-lifes who will do anything for a few coins.

If you are in need of an operation, fly home first class, the only level of service that allows you to lie flat. Never have a blood transfusion in a foreign country. Of course, if it's a matter of life or death, you have no choice. But demand screened blood.

Not many travel books talk about the unthinkable, the possibility of disease. Since this isn't just an ordinary travel book and I do talk about promiscuity, I feel it's necessary to say a few more words about sexually transmitted diseases.

Aids

Derived from a retrovirus and characterized by severe immunity deficiency resulting in opportunistic infections and malignancies, AIDS is called the human immunodeficiency virus (HIV). This retrovirus contains an enzyme called transriptase, which can convert RNA in the cytoplasm into DNA, which may then replicate and move into the cell nucleus where it becomes part of the host cell DNA. There it can alter normal cell function and cause death. During the last decade of research, over 120,000 deaths have occurred as a result of AIDS. By 1993, the death toll (cumulative over 15 years) will be about 350,000.

The oddity of this virus is that it may cause different diseases in different people and living things. AIDS attacks your weak spots; it may cause pneumonia in one person, and cancer in another. It can cause immunodeficiency disorder even in rabbits.

The epidemic first surfaced in the late 1970s, when rare cancers and uncommon infections began appearing in gay men. Now after a decade of research, some interesting findings are apparent. This is a blood to blood transmitted disease, and only 4% of newly diagnosed AIDS cases in the United States can be traced to heterosexual contact. In fact, the AIDS virus passes more easily from men to women than it does from women to men. In a recent study conducted at the University of California, Berkeley, of 307 couples divided into two groups, one in which the male had AIDS and the female did not, the other in which the female had AIDS and the male did not, only one male as opposed to 61 females subsequently contracted AIDS.

The lesson to be learned here is caution with new partners, but don't let it force you to lose that spirit of adventure that makes travel so special. The better you take care of your car the longer it lasts!! If you change the oil, the tires, the shocks, the plugs, the coolant and watch the brake lining and oil pressure, the chances of failure are reduced. More than likely when you're stuck in Las Vegas and the temperature is 110 degrees, your car won't let you down. Your body is the same way; take care of it and it will take care of you.

AIDS, like the flu, colds or infections, preys on weak bodies that are run-down, bodies in which the immunity system is busy fighting off strange bugs. When traveling, you are more susceptible to temperature changes, tiredness, different food and water bacteria, and strange germs wearing down your body's defenses. When traveling, take good care of yourself; get a good night sleep, go easy on alcohol, get moderate exercise, stick to a healthy diet, nap in the afternoon, and don't try and pretend you're a 20-year-old Don Juan who can do it all night with a multitude of partners.

In a new study at the University of Miami Medical School, (1991) men who practiced relaxation techniques or who did regular aerobic exercise had a higher blood levels of CD4 cells, the immune system cells that are attacked by the AIDS virus. Even those already infected with HIV, stayed healthier longer (maybe that explains Magic Johnson's fabulous performance in the 1992 N.B.A. All-Star game and Arthur Ashe's remarakble health after ten years of HIV and a heart operation and brain surgery.)

MORE REASONS TO WEAR A CONDOM!

Herpes AIDS kills, but genital herpes makes life miserable. A sexually transmitted disease, herpes causes painful blisters in the genital area and makes you very uncomfortable. It does not kill but more than 30 million Americans have herpes and there are as many as half a million new cases each year. There is no cure.

Herpes is transmitted by oral sex. If you've wondered why AIDS is now transmitted by heterosexual sex (supposedly impossible since AIDS virus must get into the blood system) then herpes is one of the answers! Herpes plays a big role in the transmission of HIV because in an active case of herpes there are open sores that provide a port of entry for the AIDS virus. For women this infection can cause complications at child-birth and be dangerous to the newborn.

Herpes sores are obvious, so check closely any new sexual partner. The latest study suggests that you have a 10% risk even when your partner shows *no signs* of blisters or rashes.

Syphilis Fifty million people get syphilis each year, with 400,000 in the United States. A tiny, spiral germ or spirochete, known as Treponema Pallidum, is the culprit. In acquired syphilis, the organism enters the body through the mucous membranes or skin. Within hours it reaches the regional lymph nodes and rapidly spreads throughout the body. It will attack any kind of tissue and is very contagious in its early stages. The infection is usually transmitted by genital to genital contact, but it's possible to get syphilis by oral sex as well. Syphilis can be cured easily if caught in the early stages, but if left untreated, it can be deadly.

Diagnosis: Because syphilis can mimic most skin diseases, any unusual skin eruption (remember the infection occurs where the germ entered and here creates the sore) or unexplained lesion should be considered. For the man, the main symptom is a chancre that can be single or multiple with a hard base. It will not bleed, but when opened a clear serum departs. Congenital syphilis or trichomoniasis has symptoms that are hard to detect, but usually there is a discharge early in the morning and some urethral irritation (in other words, it hurts when you pee). For women, there is a strong vaginal secretion and possibly anemia or loss of weight. An observant male can notice a certain uneasiness of the infected female. Latent syphilis in the female can possibly be detected by unusual nervousness and a shaky and illegible handwriting.

Yeast infections Commonly called genital Candidiasis, yeast infections are usually found in women but can be transmitted to men. These infections are very common especially in hot climates. When men get it, they usually complain of soreness and irritation of the penis, especially after intercourse. The infection can spread, especially in females, by normal flora or from the patient's skin. For the women, a discharge that looks like cottage cheese is common and very obvious.

Gonorrhea The organism, Neisseria gonorrhoeae, is usually spread by sexual contact. It's usually difficult for a man to tell if a woman has gonorrhea. As for the men, within two to fourteen days, a yellowish-green discharge is common. This disease usually affects the mucous membrane, especially of the sex organ, and the eyes. Generally, gonorrhea does more damage to women (especially unborn women), but left untreated it can create a painful genital infection. It is estimated that more than 250 million people worldwide and 3 million nationally are infected annually with gonorrhea.

Diagnosis: The best way to diagnose gonorrhea is is to have a lab do a gram-stained smear (almost 100% accurate for men). For women this method is only 60% accurate, and a culture is needed for proper identification.

Hepatitis HBV, compared to AIDS, is 100 times more contagious and one million times more concentrated in the blood. Hepatitis can live at room temperature for as long as a week while the AIDS virus dies shortly after exposure. Over 300,000 Americans per year contract the Hepatitis B virus and 10% become chronic carriers. Of the more than 200 million chronic HBV carriers, 2 million will die of liver disease. HBV-related liver cancer is the most common form of cancer and the ninth leading cause of death worldwide. The virus is transmitted in body fluids, such as saliva and blood. It is most commonly transmitted through sex and lives in the seamen and vaginal fluids. The real problem is that this virus is symptomless and you may never know you are infected! You become fatigued, may have a slight fever, nausea and loss of appetite. The good news is that there is an easy and successful vaccine that is almost 100% effective. If for some strange reason you don't expect to use a condom in your travels, a vaccine booster is a good idea for those lustful adventures.

Fungus Why is it that only men get this infection? Do we cover our feet too much or sweat more between our toes? When I'm in a hot climate, I often get this infection: microscopic skin fungi, called dermatophytes, enter the small cracks or fissures and start to multiply. Once in Caracas, Venezuela, I got a bad case and had a difficult time describing my problem to the druggist. Finally, I took off my shoe and put my toe in his face and got immediate treatment.

Liquid treatment is the best, as it doesn't rub off and is just as effective as cream. Powders and aerosols are worthless. Always remember to dry your feet, wear sandals, live in all cotton, and wash your clothes often. Always carry a treatment with you.

TRAVELING IN GOOD HEALTH

Perhaps a good philosophy in meeting new sexual partners is our "used-car analogy". Don't buy a car without thoroughly examining it and once parked in your garage, periodic inspections are wise. Don't take any long trips before you have complete confidence in the reliability of your vehicle. Prolonged relationships with an infected partner can be deadly! Don't fall for the "little old lady in Pasadena only drove it to the store once a week" hype.

If a new acquittance swears that you are her "first," be suspicious. Remember, women are at least ten times more susceptible to HIV than men and if she doesn't care or feigns ignorance, then I'd be worried!

There is a different method of treating venereal disease outside the United States. There are not as many doctors, hospitals or clinics. In Brazil, Thailand, Mexico, and most of South America, the pharmacist is your doctor. You won't need a prescription for many drugs; the druggist can hand you penicillin on the spot. It is important to describe the nature of your problem clearly. You may need to recruit the bell-boy who speaks the local dialect. In the hard-core sex centers of the world, there will always be clinics that only deal with venereal disease; just open the paper or ask your trusted bell-boy. For a tip he will probably personally escort you to his favorite.

I'm not trying to frighten you, but according to Murphy's Law, if it's possible, it will happen. My rules for playing and staying healthy are: practice *safe sex*, don't believe in the *"Virgin Mary,"* don't be embarrassed to say *NO*, and don't act impulsively--*think*.

Medicines to Carry

Actually in all my travels I have never had any medical problems. I did get bad cases of the flu--once in Phuket, and once landing in Hawaii after a trip to the Philippines. Have you ever noticed how many types of flu are named after an Asian country? In Hawaii it was called the Philippine flu, and in Phuket it was the Hong Kong flu. What isn't available over the counter in local drugstores in foreign countries are our great new flu medicines, so remember to pack a good flu and cold medicine like Thera Flu.

Other recommended medicinal aids for long trips are a good supply of Ibuprofen (Advil or Nuprin are great for everything from headaches to tennis elbow), big and small band-aids (I always cut or bleed at the worst possible times), a few ear plugs for those noisy hotel neighbors or diving (ear aches are painful when flying), and a good bug repellent. If someone tries to tell you that Pepto-Bismo is old-fashioned, don't believe it. I've tried them all for that upset stomach and nausea -- nothing works better. The liquid is better than the tablets and now comes in easy-to-carry plastic bottles.

A NOTE ABOUT SMOKING

While the death toll from AIDS is dreadful, I want to put things in perspective. Last year there were 157,000 lung cancer deaths, and a new study, reported in the Journal of National Cancer Institute (9/91) maintains that smoking was the major cause in 91.5% of these deaths and that, for the male, the risk of dying from lung cancer has doubled in the last three decades. In the findings of the January 1992 Journal of Public Health, it was reported that 30% of all cancers and 85% of lung cancer in the U.S. would have been avoided if current smokers had never smoked. This was based on a 20 year study of 8,000 Japanese-American men who smoked one pack a day. The American Cancer Society says there will be one million new cases this year and *half will die.*

In one year as many people die from smoking as have died from AIDS in the last 15 years. AIDS is surely a deadly epidemic, but that guy blowing smoke in your face at the bar is killing you too. No matter how sexually active you are, your chance of dying from smoking is greater (unless you practice unsafe sex). Statistics tell us that it's more dangerous to sit continuously next to a habitual smoker than it is is to have un-protected sex with a stranger. A 1991 study of the American Heart Association's Journal Circulation found that second-hand smoke caused an estimated 37,000 heart disease deaths per year among non-smokers in the United States; there is a direct link between second-hand smoke and the narrowing of the arteries.

Most importantly, a recent Boston University study of young impotent men found that men who smoke a pack a day for five years are 15 percent more likely than non-smokers to develop clogged arteries in the penis, which in turn can cause impotence.

An unusual approach to solving the smoking epidemic is being initiated by Singapore, where the government has created a smoking ban that includes banks, barber shops, taxis, private buses and a fine up to $600 and even a $300 penalty if you light up in cinemas, fast food outlets, public buses, subways, government oﬁices, stores, and indoor sports arenas. Smokers can light up only in bars during the hours of no food service! The smoking lobby in the United States would go crazy with such laws, but how else to end the greatest threat to "male health".

I believe that the warning label on cigarettes should read: "smoking is more dangerous than AIDS."

A GUIDE TO MAKING

YOUR OWN RESERVATIONS

TOLL-FREE (1-800) NUMBERS

DOMESTIC AIRLINES

Alaska	426-0333
American	433-7300
Delta	323-2323
Northwest	225-2525
TWA	221-2000
United	241-6522
Continental	525-0280

FOREIGN AIRLINES

Cathay	233-2742
China Air	227-5118
Korean Air	421-8200
Malaysian	421-8642
Japan Air	525-3663
A.N.A.	235-9262
Thai Air	426-5204
Singapore	742-3333
Varig	468-2744
VASP	732-vasp

Trans-Brazil 272-7458

Mexicana 531-7921

HOTELS

Hilton 445-8667

Holiday Inn 465-4329

Hyatt 233-1234

Shangri-La 942-5050

Marriott 288-9290

Grand Hyatt 228-9000

Radisson 333-3333

Sheraton 325-3535

Stouffer 268-3571

Ritz Carlton 241-3333

Westin 521-2000

Meridien 543-4300

Ramada 228-2828

Leading Hotels of the World 223-6800

Regent 545-4000

Omni 843-6664

Preferred Hotels 323-7500

World Inter-Continental 327-0200

CAR RENTALS

Alamo 462-5266

Avis 331-1212

Budget 527-0700

Dollar 800-4000

Hertz 654-3131

Thrifty 367-2277

National 227-7368

Enterprise 325-8007

JOIN THE CLUB:

FREQUENT FLYERS AND

THE AIRLINES

American Advantage At 10,000 miles, you get a free
upgrade to first class; at 20,000 miles, a free coach ticket in
the United States; at 65,000 miles, a ticket to Asia on a
partner airline. American has just purchased new routes to
South America and Europe.

Partners Avis, Hertz, Cathay Pacific, Quantas, British
Airways, Forum Hotels, Sheraton, Wydham Hotels, MCI.
New program with City Bank; join the credit card program
and get one mile credit per dollar spent with no limit (1-
800-FLY-4444)

Phone: 1-800-433-7300

Northwest Perks At 20,000 miles you get a free coach
ticket in the United States; at 40,000 miles, a ticket to
Europe; and at 50,000 miles, a free coach ticket to Asia.
Many promotional rates are tied into a mileage program and
the American Express program. Possibly the best bet for
1992. Combination of Europe/Asia network plus 25%
bonus in Business class and 50% in First class with buyout
of Midway and buy in of Hawaiian Air extending your
options.

Partners: Alaska Airlines, Avis, Hertz, Hyatt, Marriott,
Radisson, Budget.

Phone: .... 1-800-777-8585.

Pan-Am Expired November 1, 1991. All excess miles will be transferred to Delta's program. If you have a Pan-Am coupon, it expires one year from the date issued, and tickets from this coupon are good for one year after issued. You then have two years to use up miles on the **old** mileage award basis. Delta requires almost **double** the mileage for the same trips. These coupons are valuable, for a 30,000-mile coupon will get you a round-trip to Brazil.

Phone: 1-800-348-8000 or 1-800-221-1111

Delta At 40,000 miles, you get one free round-trip for North America or the Caribbean. At 70,000 miles, you get a free round-trip to Europe. For any flight (even 100 miles), you are credited with 1,000 miles. Same credit of 1,000 miles for car rental or hotel partner.

DELTA WILL HONOR PAN-AM CERTIFICATES TO EUROPE AND PAN-AM EXCESS MILES WILL BE PUT INTO A DELTA CLUB PROGRAM.

Partners: Alamo, Hertz, National, Marriott Hotel, Preferred Hotels, and Trusthouse Forte Hotels.

Phone: 1-800-323-2323

Continental One Pass For 10,000 miles you can upgrade from coach in the U.S.; for 20,000 miles, you get one free U. S. round-trip ticket; for 30,000 miles, a ticket to Hawaii; and for 35,000, a round-trip to Europe.

Partners: Air France, Lufthansa, National, Thrifty, Marriott Doubletree Hotels, Radisson Hotels, Camino Real Hotels (best Mexican chain).

Phone: 1-800-525-0280

United Mileage Plus For 20,000 miles, you get one free round-trip in the United States, Canada, or Mexico, and 50% hotel and car-rental discounts; for 75,000 miles a free business-class ticket to Asia or Europe. As of January 1, 1992 will **not** honor Pan-Am miles.

Partners: Pan-Am, Westin Hotels, Hilton, Hyatt Hotels, Alamo and Hertz. Cruise on the Holland America line and earn 1,000 miles per night.

Phone: 1-800-421-4635

Appendix

ADDITIONAL NOTES For a flyer who takes frequent short flights, Delta is the best; all minimum flight and partner usage is 1,000 miles. With Pan-Am now gone, the most generous and comprehensive is Continental One Pass. This program allows you to upgrade from coach excursion within the 48 states for 10,000 miles For the long distance traveller Northwest is the best, allowing upgrades from cheap economy to Business for 30,000 miles (United and American is 40,000). Remember, you can't credit two club accounts at once; you must choose. If you check into a hotel partner, have it credited to your airline frequent flyer account, not the hotel's, if you want to maximize free flights. Also, most hotel and car rentals must be made in conjunction with your flight for proper credit. The norm is within 24 hours, but this can vary. A great new program is American Express Frequent Flyer account, in which all purchases can be credited towards seven different airlines. How would you like to take a free seven-day, self-drive tour of Germany in a new Porsche, with accommodations in medieval castles? A mere $175,000 charge on your Gold Card and it's free.

HOTELS

Marriott Honored Guests You get a 3,000-mile enroll-ment bonus and 1,000 points per night or 500 miles toward the partner airline of your choice. You need 20,000 points for a free night, so airline miles, I feel, are more valuable.

Benefits: Check cashing, priority reservations, free newspaper and use of fitness gym, room upgrade, and special phone number for reservations and car rental discounts.

Phone: 1-800-228-9290

Sheraton Club International You get 500 bonus points for enrolling. Your $25 yearly fee can be paid by points. Free awards include an answering machine at 5,000 points, an Apple Image Writer at 50,000 points. Travelers can credit to only one program per stay (airline or gifts). Club points can be converted to American Airline at 10,000 points for 7,500 miles. You get four points per dollar spent.

Benefits: Upgrades when available, late check out, newspaper and numerous auto rental discounts.

Phone: 1-800-247-2582

Hyatt Gold Passport Enrollment bonus of 1,000 points. Members earn five points per dollar spent. When you rent a car from Avis or Budget, you get a 300 point bonus. You can earn simultaneous air and hotel credit with partners Northwest or Delta. With 8,000 points, you can get one free weekend night at a hotel or resort. With 100,000 points you get eight free nights in a suite, one free, round-trip, companion air ticket and a full-size car for four weekend nights. A new Gold Passport program allows you to buy booklets of five "upgrade coupons" for $125. Each $25 coupon is good for a confirmed upgrade to a suite or concierge floor at any of the 152 Hyatts world-wide, including resorts. A new Gold Passport program allows you to buy 173 booklets of five "upgrade coupons" for $125. Each $25 coupon is good for a confirmed upgrade to a suite or concierge floor at any of the 152 Hyatts world-wide, including resorts.

Benefits: Express check-in and -out, special gold-floor (separate check-in from the hotel sand personal business services), free coffee, newspaper, and use of fitness center.

Phone: 1-800-544-9288

Holiday Inn Priority Club You pay a one-time fee of $10. You may redeem points for domestic or international vacations. You get 6,000 points for a round trip in the U. S. on Northwest. Members earn one point per dollar spent. For a $100 Holiday Inn guest certificate, you get 2100 points and two free weekend rentals from Hertz.

Benefits: Guaranteed, single-corporate rate, free upgrade, extended check-out to 2:00 p.m., Hertz rental-car discounts, and 25% bonus on airline mileage credits.

Phone: 1-800-654-6852

Appendix

Hilton Honors Members earn ten points per dollar charged. Enrollment bonus of 2,000 points and 3,000 additional points if first stay is within 60 days of enrollment. You pay no fee, and guests who arrive on partner airline (United, TWA, U.S. Air) receive a 25% bonus. For 15,000 points, you get one free weekend night at a hotel or resort; for 150,000, a free ticket to Asia or Europe.

Benefits: Free stay for your spouse, expedited check-in and -out, free newspaper, reservation priorities and special phone number.

Phone: 1-800-446-6677

It should be noted that the benefits, methods and amounts of points awarded for stays changes monthly. Call for current information.

CAR RENTALS

Avis Wizard Club Free Wizard Number allows corporate rate, automatic reservations with computer knowledge of your car preference. Avis Express picks you up at the airport terminal and delivers you directly to your G. M. car. Always ask for AAA discount if you belong to this club. Remember, cars are always cheaper on the long weekend rate. Cars must be returned by Monday midnight, or higher rates apply. 1-800-831-8000

Hertz #1 Club Free express service number allows you to go directly to Express check-in with advance reservations. You get corporate rate with "Gold Club." Annual $50 charge for the Gold Club, and your car is waiting for you with trunk open, air-conditioning or heater on, and rental contract on the dash. Ford products are featured. 1-800-654-3131

TIPS ABOUT TRAVEL CLUBS

Pick one club to stay with; for example, if you choose Continental One Pass, at 20,000 miles (no deductions) you get free a one-class upgrade for every 10,000 miles, first-class check in, priority baggage handling and priority boarding (you board with the first-class passengers, a great deal if you're carrying on all your luggage).

Don't call on Mondays, and make your reservations early if using mileage awards for tickets. It took me a month of calls to get the correct flight to Asia on United; they call it "capacity control:" only a small percentage of seats are allowed for free travel, and they go fast. Use free tickets wisely; if you use a companion coupon or award, make sure the paid ticket is yours so you get the mileage. Free tickets don't receive frequent flyer miles. Recently my summer trip to Spain was free because I sold a companion ticket to my friend, offering him a 20% discount under the normal price so he couldn't refuse. I paid for mine, and they credited me with triple miles, which in turn paid for my next trip to Brazil.

If you have to choose between hotel points or air miles, take the air miles, as their awards will include free auto rentals and up to a 50% hotel discount.

You don't have to fly at all to receive air miles. Most airlines sponsor credit cards and all charges are credited as mileage; usually you get one mile per dollar charged. Pick one charge card and stay with it.

Be aware that some frequent flyer certificates have expiration dates. A practical (economical) solution exists, if you can't use your miles in time, in the classified of large metropolitan papers - sell them to individuals, travel agents or businesses looking for miles. Remember the closer you get to the expiration date, the less valuable the miles. Short a few miles for that upgrade - purchase the miles the same way you sell, but shop around for the best prices and use a credit card for purchases.

Appendix

If you follow these simple rules and join the clubs, most travelling can be fun and spontaneous. Carrying on your luggage and having your rental car ready, keys in the ignition, means that by the time most people are trying to figure out which carousel their luggage is on, you are already on the freeway or checked into your hotel and on the beach, missing all the confusion and long lines.

We are interested in hearing about your travel experiences. We invite you to write to us at:

TSM Publishing

Suite 122

3600 S. Harbor Blvd.

Channel Island, CA 93035

If you are interested in subscribing to our newsletter please contact us at the above address for a free sample.